Carol Duval

Trying Lives

A House Sitter's Tale

Published in 2019 by FeedARead.com Publishing
Copyright © Carol Duval

A CIP catalogue record for this title is available from the British Library.

But wherever friendly paths intersect,
the whole world looks like home, for a time.

~ Hermann Hesse, *Demian*

Contents

FIRST THOUGHTS

1. Synchronicity

Here I was, sipping a coffee on a cool veranda in Nimbin, Australia's hippy homeland, skimming the New York Times and taking in the tats, dreadlocks, retro '60s Indian skirts and straggly beards of the locals.

My husband Richard and I were spending a couple of weeks looking after some chickens and a duck called Max on a lushly planted farmlet in the nearby Nightcap Ranges. For a while I'd been pondering the idea of turning my travel blog of the last couple of years into something more substantial but had kept putting it off. This wasn't just bog-standard procrastination but because of what I felt was a brick-wall structural problem — caused mainly by Donald Trump.

The trouble was that over recent years my experiences of the places where we've stayed have been coloured more and more by the daily news which, let's face it, has been pretty weird. Mass migrations, the Brexit debacle, Russian overreach, Donald Trump's head-snapping, ugly rallies — it's been one heck of a ride.

It's also becoming very clear that as much as I value travel, there's a huge price to pay. Mass travel really is a two-edged sword. Travel broadens the mind and enriches the spirit but it also brings over-crowding, tacky souvenir shops and inflated real estate prices with so many short-term rentals now available through sites like Airbnb and FlipKey. Oscar Wilde was dead right when he said we always kill the thing we love.

So if instead of simply recounting memories of places and people I'd encountered while travelling, I were to write a memoir that was a more fulsome reflection of my experiences, I'd need to include some philosophical musing, which wouldn't be quite so straightforward.

By this time I'd pretty well given up on the idea of writing a book at all. That is until, fingers sticky from the organic, gluten-free orange cake now wiped clean, I was able to check my New York Times newsfeed. One of my favourite columnists, Gail Collins, had written a very funny piece, 'Our Gold-Leaf Presidency', satirising Trump's grandiose taste in domestic architecture and comparing his Florida resort Mar-a-Lago to 'a cathedral on psychedelic drugs'.

Sitting there among the hippies at the Armonica Café in Nimbin, home to the 1973 Aquarius Festival and famed for its main street's psychedelic murals and weed peddlers, that paragraph seemed in some weird way to be speaking to me. And I hadn't even tried the widely available 'adult cookies' yet!

I try to live in a reality-based universe so dismissed this thought as nothing more than an amusing coincidence and wandered over the road to check out the Information Centre. After rummaging through the crystals, knitting and woodwork on sale, I noticed a poster advertising the upcoming Nimbin MardiGrass. And there, stuck in the bottom corner, below a head-banded, dreadlocked Prime Minister Malcolm Turnbull, was a second sign.

Squeezed in at the bottom corner was the image of a fierce, red-faced Donald Trump smoking a huge joint, announcing the MardiGrass website.

Hmmm.... This was starting to feel a little, well, magic-mushroomy spooky.

Somewhat bemused, I looked up and there at the back of the room in three-dimensional splendour, stood a huge wooden signpost — the Nimbin Pole — with its arms pointing to typical New-Agey places like Bliss Lane, Cynics and Black Magicians. And there, right at the top, was the clincher.

Synchronicity.

The Cosmos had spoken thrice. No more excuses. Get on with that book!

2. From Seeing to Being

Two of our favourite pet-sitting assignments were at opposite ends of the world, looking after two completely different types of animals. One was a black cat, Merlin, and the other, the aforementioned white duck, Max. Not only were they different in fur and feather but they also had completely different personalities.

Merlin's home was a converted barn atop a high hill looking out over rolling farmland and woods near the Welsh/English border. Merlin passed his days, and a fair chunk of his evenings, roaming the surrounding orchards, fields and vegetable gardens. He was an adventurer — curious and carefree.

Max's home was on that farmlet near Nimbin deep in the subtropical rainforest of Australia's east coast, near the NSW/Queensland border. Max passed his days searching for food — nights were spent in the safety of his shed — never venturing far beyond the path that led from his water bowl to the chicken coop on the far side of the lawn. He was a homebody — comfortable and cautious.

While sitting on the veranda one afternoon watching Max poking about in the grass as he awaited his regular 4 p.m. bread snack, it occurred to me that much of my travelling has been a little bit Max and a little bit Merlin.

There's the impulse for adventure — Merlin — but also a yearning for the safety and comfort of home — Max. I think this is a pretty common experience actually. How often do we all come home from our travels, exhilarating as they were, and delight in the relief of sleeping in our own beds and knowing where to find all our stuff? To love the buzz of roaming like Merlin yet welcome the restfulness of home and nesting like Max?

It struck me too, that over the years I've begun to view the whole travel experience differently. When I started travelling, I was in search of adventure. After all those years in school and then establishing a career, I did what so many young Australians did at that time. I headed to the UK for a year, working part-time, backpacking around Europe on a Eurail pass and staying in youth hostels. That's how Richard and I first met — waiting on a platform in Copenhagen for the overnight train to Oslo.

Not having travelled much further than Australia and New Zealand at that point but with family in England, I wanted to see the 'old country' and meet my relatives. I wanted to see London where my mother grew up and lived through the blitz before she upped stakes, married a Kiwi soldier and moved to New Zealand.

But I was also keen to visit the places I'd read about in my Early English university studies. I wanted to see for myself the Viking ruins in Denmark, King Arthur's legendary birthplace in Cornwall and the Sutton Hoo treasures in the British Museum.

As for Richard, he was more of a free spirit and just wanted to see how far his Eurail pass could take him in his four weeks' leave from the US Air Force. But he did have something of a bucket list of things to see — places, monuments and art works — suggested by that '70s tourist guidebook and frugal travellers' bible, *Europe on $5 a Day*.

~

But now there's a difference. As I've grown older and with the growing realisation that life is short and getting shorter, I want to go a bit further than just having adventures and discovering what's out there. No longer content with following tour guides' must-see bucket lists or even the more scholarly paths determined by my university studies, I'd rather have more personal, immersive experiences.

With my career behind me, I was now free to indulge in some musing and philosophising and especially to explore the age-old philosophical question: What is the 'good life'? But discovering what makes for a life well lived also means thinking about its opposite. What makes for a life *badly* lived? Were there universal principles underpinning how to live well — or badly?

In *The Art of Travel*, philosopher Alain de Botton describes stopping by a red door of an apartment building in Amsterdam and immediately being seized by a desire to live there for the rest of his life. Simply imagining living in that net-curtained apartment with its bicycle resting against the wall wasn't enough. He desperately wanted, in that moment, to *be* that unknown Amsterdam apartment-dwelling, bicycle-riding person and to live that person's life.

In this vignette, de Botton struck at the heart of my particular travel bug. Travel is a way of getting a taste of a completely different lifestyle, though here he was suggesting he wanted more than a mere taste. He wanted a full-blown feast.

It was this impulse that prompted me to explore ways of staying longer than just a couple of days as a tourist and that would allow enough time to try living as some other person in some other place. By staying on their patch, surrounded by their belongings and rubbing shoulders with their neighbours, I'd be as close as I could get to trying another life.

What would it be like living in an English village, a remote Spanish farmhouse, a French château, a Dutch townhouse? Could such experiences teach me something about what makes for a good life? And how many such lives could I cram into one?

Quite a few, as it turned out, including all the above.

So for the nuts and bolts of this experiment.

Richard and I wanted to be low-impact travellers, trying out different lifestyles and perhaps gaining new insights along the way.

Once we knew our goals, we needed a workable, inexpensive plan. This meant we had to find a way of staying in different places for reasonable periods of time while also being sensitive to our impact on both the environment and the host communities. We didn't want to add to the damage already inflicted by mass tourism. This was a tall order and might not always be possible but we'd certainly try our best.

The least invasive way of doing this we decided would be through house swapping, house sitting or low-impact renting. By living in someone else's home in these ways, we'd not be depriving the locals of valuable accommodation and we'd only rent if we could let out our own home at the same time.

But which of these might be the best way to start our new experiment in travel? How best to allow space for our adventurous cat-like Merlin spirits to roam while also honouring the nesting impulses of Max the duck?

My Max nature won out. We'd begin cautiously by keeping as closely to a sense of 'home' as possible.

The answer was house swapping.

TESTING
THE WATERS

3.   Flood, Fire and Torches on the Thames

Like many people today, Richard and I have lived in many different places for work or to be near family, mainly the US, UK and Australia. Exciting as this might sound, it can be something of a two-edged sword. When you spend a lot of time in more than one place, make friends and begin to feel a sense of belonging, it can become hard to settle for too long in one without missing the other. It's such a common phenomenon that there's now a name for people like us: 'ping-pongers'.

That's why our first foray into house swapping was geared towards the UK. It had the advantage of not only ping-ponging us back to a country we knew well and were starting to miss but also offered loads of potential for a European escapade.

So how to go about it? House exchange websites make it pretty easy to find loads of potential swaps but there are still plenty of challenges.

One downside to living 'down under' in Australia but wanting to find a swap in the Northern Hemisphere, is working around the opposite seasons. It's not that difficult to find northerners keen to swap their dark cold winter for an Australian summer but not so easy the other way around. That's the situation we found ourselves in when searching for our first exchange. The choice was to go in the northern winter or not at all. So — decision made!

Another potential problem is finding a fellow swapper whose idea of comfort and cleanliness matches your own. We saw any number of listings where the location and timing were spot-on, but the places themselves looked unappealing — cluttered and messy, staid and boring, poky and confining. Knowing we'd be living there for a fair chunk of time, we wanted to feel comfortable and not desperate to escape the minute we arrived. That did actually happen once but more on that later.

From the listings posted on an exchange website, we found what looked like a contender in Goring-upon-Thames, an area that appealed as it was relatively close to our old haunts in Berkshire. The home looked similar to our own with pared-back yet comfortable Scandinavian furnishings, not surprising since our potential swap partner, Hanna, was Danish. So after a few emails and Skype chats we all felt good enough about living in each other's homes to prepare ourselves for our first home swap.

We'd have a home base for the two months of the exchange so would have ample time to get to know the village and take part in its Christmas activities and we could invite friends to visit as if in our own home. But we'd also have the opportunity to venture further afield with some relatively inexpensive travel in nearby Europe. This first experience actually turned out to be such a success that it's been our model for house swapping and sitting ever since.

I have to admit that we were extremely lucky with the handover. One of Hanna's sons was already living in Sydney so that made the keys' handover easy. But better still, another of her sons, who'd later join her in Sydney, came to Heathrow in the cold drizzle of a pre-dawn December morning to pick us up in his car — included in the exchange — and drove us all the way to Goring. Well, it was easy for us but not for him. After battling London's early morning traffic, getting stuck in a road diversion just outside Goring, finally arriving at the house and lugging our bags upstairs, he had to walk to the train station to catch a crowded commuter train back to London, leaving us to get acquainted with what would be our home for the next two months.

The townhouse was in a wide cul-de-sac so it was fairly easy to meet the neighbours. I've never understood why there's this stereotype of the English being cold and unfriendly. This has never been our experience and Goring was no exception. Most of the neighbours quickly introduced themselves and made us feel very welcome.

Goring certainly was a great choice for our first exchange. It's relatively sheltered from wind by the Chiltern Hills — though not from flood as we soon discovered — and has a great sense of community. Being on the main train line to London and Oxford was another plus.

The River Thames separates Goring from its sister village Streatley, the short walk from one to the other being across a pretty bridge anchored by the perpetually crowded, trendy Pierrepont's café on the Goring side and the posh Swan country hotel on the Streatley side. The bridge turned out to be the hub of the village, what with the café's delicious cakes and the abundance of things to look at — the old mill, the lock and masses of swans, ducks and geese revelling in the deep, cold water of the weir below. It was also a good spot to get an unobtrusive look at (the now late) George Michael's house and garden that ran down to the riverbank.

❧

Walking is the best way to get to know an area and Goring certainly wasn't short of places to walk. Being early December though, this meant bundling up in loads of layers before heading out into the cold, wind and rain.

One morning after a particularly stormy night, we came across an elderly gentleman, very properly attired in a three-piece suit, holding up his fence that had been blown down in the gales. Politely rejecting our offer of help he stood there, still propping up the fence and being buffeted by wind, all the while engaging us in a jolly conversation. Where we were from? Why we were in Goring and how long would we be staying? And how lucky we were to be here in time for the Christmas Eve torchlight procession! Our ears pricked up. Well, he added, it *is* a little bit pagan, what with the torches and all, but it's jolly good fun with the procession through the village and then carolling — not exactly by candlelight — but by torchlight, and everyone really looks forward to it each year.

This torchlight procession was sounding more intriguing by the minute. Visions came to mind of flower-bedecked villagers of Summerisle, that fictional Scottish village made famous in the '60s movie *The Wicker Man*, gleefully singing and dancing round the soon-to-be cremated 'outsider' trapped inside a giant wicker effigy. There was no way we'd miss it.

For the next two weeks we entered into the Christmas spirit by going on loads of muddy Thameside walks; slipping and sliding along tracks and trails through the surrounding Chiltern Hills; visiting Christmas markets in the nearby towns of Wallingford, Oxford and

Cheltenham; and meeting friends at our favourite shop in the whole world, Daylesford Farm Shop in the Cotswolds.

Forget the glitz and glitter of Harrods and Harvey Nicks or the bright lights and designer fashions of Oxford Street and Piccadilly Circus. Rather, give me the soft, grey-timbered barns of misty Daylesford with their mounds of purple kale and Brussels sprouts, spicy Christmas candles and the fragrance of freshly cut flowers artfully arranged in zinc buckets on the flagstone floors. Sure, a takeaway organic carrot and kale salad would set you back a pretty penny, and don't even think about one of those super-fine cashmere, pastel-coloured sweaters. But we could never resist splashing out on a coffee and fruit toast in the shabby-chic café overlooking the gravelled courtyard and fields beyond.

What with all those muddy Chilterns walks and window-shopping trips, not to mention the Christmassy scents of rustic yet expensively elegant cinnamon and dried orange wreaths, it behoved us to try those very English winter specialities: mulled wine, mulled cider and craft beers. Since we were in an English village, and a well-heeled one at that, there was a goodly selection of pubs, as well as the high-end Swan over the bridge in Streatley. Although we never did manage to rub shoulders with George Michael, who was living there at the time, the local barmen told us tales of his regular appearances and how he was treated just like any other villager. It was interesting to hear too that he'd been a great supporter of the torchlight procession in the past. We couldn't wait.

In the days before Christmas Eve and the (hopefully) pagan, procession, we noticed that many of the local shops were stocking the aforementioned torches — strange objects that we'd never seen before or have seen since — and we couldn't work out how they'd escaped the UK's usual stringent health and safety regulations. They'd looked dodgy in the shops and on Christmas Eve, when rugged up in our thickest, warmest jackets but sadly sans torch, we headed off to join the procession, we realised just how dodgy they really were.

The procession was certainly impressive. It seemed like the whole village was on the move, wielding flaming torches as they made their way down the narrow pavements to the open ground beside the church. There, behind a low fence, was a huge bonfire. This was indeed starting to look quite promisingly pagan. But that's as pagan as it got and thankfully the bonfire remained a nonhuman-fuelled focus of warmth and fun.

Photocopied carol sheets in hand, we tried getting into the Christmas spirit by singing along with our fellow villagers but being torchless ourselves, found it nigh impossible to read the words. We tried edging towards torched-up groups without looking too pushy — after all, we weren't entirely integrated into the village yet — but I ended up copping a cinder and burning a hole in my new jacket. At that point I again wondered briefly about health and safety issues but what the heck! At least it wasn't my eye and a burn hole in my jacket was a small price to pay for such an enjoyable evening's entertainment.

I've since discovered that the torchlight procession has now been cancelled, at least for the time being, a victim of its own popularity, with so many non-villagers swelling the numbers to dangerous levels. As swappers we can rest easy as we were only displacing people who'd normally be there anyway. Actually, our impact was insignificant compared to the impact it left on my jacket.

Happily for us, Christmas Day turned out to be one of the clearest, finest days of our two-month stay. It's always a bit of a challenge cooking in someone else's kitchen, so on this house swap I tended to go for easy-to-prepare casseroles or bakes when entertaining friends and Marks and Spencer's takeaways when cooking for ourselves. For Christmas, I'd bought an assortment of such dishes so we knew we'd have a very easy and relaxing time of it.

We began with a gentle walk along the Thames path, still muddy from all the rain, to the next village, the picturesque South Stoke with its neat thatched cottages and the popular Perch and Pike pub, perfect for a warming mulled wine. Being such a pleasant day, we met many of the local children trying out their new Christmas bikes on the rutted river path and along the quiet village roads. Once home, as the day was drawing in, we feasted on our easy-to-prepare smoked salmon, ham, roast sweet potatoes, spicy red cabbage and Christmas pudding with custard.

Just as well we'd made the most of that crisp, sunny day because the next morning the heavens opened and it didn't stop raining until we left the country. With 'no-drama' Obama still in the White House and Brexit not even a blip on anyone's radar, the news of the day was dominated by a non-political event — massive flooding in the UK and across swathes or Europe. As the Thames rose higher, our daily walks became ever more fascinating as we watched the water creep up the lawns of the Swan, into the boat sheds on the banks of the weir and over much of the Thames pathway. The swans, geese and ducks were in their element but many of the objects we saw being carried downstream by the muddy waters were not — heavy wooden picnic tables, boats and huge branches.

Apart from watching the waters rising, going on ever-muddier walks down the bits of river pathways that were still accessible and taking refuge in the village pubs, we began investigating a short-break escape. The flooding was interesting in its way, especially since we personally weren't in any danger of inundation. But with only a few weeks left, we wanted to do something other than battling gales and wading through mud puddles. We needed to find somewhere to roam that was relatively close, with the chance of better weather but not too pricey.

Our choice was Lisbon.

4. Flood, Fire and Tarts on the Tagus

Just like Goring, Lisbon turned out to be an excellent choice but it didn't start out that way. The night we arrived it had been raining solidly for weeks. The surf along the coast was tempestuous and the city sodden. Our informative taxi driver had tried to lift our spirits by giving us tips for our few days here but when he pulled up outside what we expected to be our Airbnb apartment — we broke our rule on this occasion I'm afraid — his optimism wilted. The address we'd given him was correct but the building looked more like a crumbling office block than apartments. Leaving us to keep dry in the taxi, he braved the downpour to check whether all was above board.

All was well and after the shock of thinking we'd been conned and were temporarily homeless, we gratefully bade our taxi driver farewell and followed our Airbnb host upstairs. After some multiple-door opening with a set of heavy antique keys, we entered a warm, bright apartment tastefully furnished by Ikea. All was indeed well. The ugly duckling façade was merely disguising its swan-like interior and Commerce Square, tram stops and the River Tagus were just steps away.

But — the food! Apologies to any Portuguese readers but we failed dismally in our efforts to find a tasty meal in Lisbon. The sardines, custard tarts, port and almonds were all pretty good but apart from these, it was all boiled potatoes, limp vegetables and bland cod. Maybe we were just unlucky with our restaurant choices but I'm afraid we weren't over-excited by our encounters with Portuguese cuisine. Back in the '80s when we lived in Hong Kong we often spent weekends in Macau where we fell in love with

Portuguese chicken so we'd had high hopes for Lisbon. Sadly though, despite our best efforts, it eluded us.

Still, everything else about Lisbon was wonderful, especially when the rain stopped, the skies cleared and we found ourselves in what seemed like a mild Sydney or San Francisco winter.

Travelling around Lisbon proved to be relatively easy with its excellent tram and train network but walking around this beautiful city with its patterned cobblestone paving and many pedestrian streets and squares was a joy.

Our favourite tram ride was to Belém, home of the rightly famous Portuguese custard tart bakery, Pastéis de Belém. I'd been trying to learn a bit of Portuguese, which turned out to be a rather difficult language, mainly because of the counter-intuitive spelling and pronunciation, so I hadn't made much progress. However, I did manage to learn how to ask for *dois café e dois pastéis de Belém por favor* though I soon needed to change the number of tarts from *dois* to *quatros*. Those little beauties were too delicious to stop at just one.

The bakery was actually a series of blue-and-white-tiled rooms filled with little marble-topped tables and with a huge kitchen right in the middle where you could watch the tarts being made through wrap-around glass windows. The story goes that a couple of centuries ago some local nuns who used egg whites to starch their veils, came up with the recipe as a way of dealing with all those leftover yolks. And thank heavens they did because we'd be all the poorer without their heavenly creations. Here's hoping that the pastry shop doesn't fall victim to its own success, like Goring's torchlight procession. It certainly seemed to be well and truly on the tour-bus trail from the number of tart-triers we saw being unloaded outside and pouring in through the doors.

One interesting thing we noticed in Lisbon was what seemed to be a certain amount of historical minimisation going on. It wasn't exactly revisionism because the more disreputable events in Portugal's history weren't hidden away but they didn't seem to feature as prominently as I would have expected.

Portugal certainly has a lot to be proud of when it comes to its maritime history and there's a monument celebrating this beside the Tagus, not far from the tart shop in Belém. This Monument to the Discoveries is shaped like a ship's prow with statues of those shipbuilders, sailors, explorers and monks, led by Henry the Navigator, all looking expectantly out to sea.

But the bit that seemed to be missing from this optimistic story was the toll their arrival took on the native peoples who were devastated in quick order by European diseases, dispossession and enslavement. It was hard to reconcile those carvings of monks, sailors and explorers, supposedly celebrating an admirable quality of the human spirit — that quest for knowledge and discovery — with the greed and sheer cruelty that went with it.

It was a similar story at the Lisbon City Museum, which, despite the rather dull name, offered a fascinating experience, both sensory as well as intellectual. We walked through life-sized reconstructions of medieval city scenes with their noisy markets and workshops, as well as the explorers' cramped ships' interiors. We felt the rumbling of the great Lisbon earthquake and saw images of the ensuing tsunami and the destruction wrought by fires that burned for days afterwards. We did see some references to the South American atrocities but they seemed somewhat brief and not as prominently displayed as I would have expected, considering their huge historical significance.

In the same way there was little reference to the Inquisition in this museum or elsewhere. Not far from our apartment on Lisbon's vast riverside square, for example, was the site of the 1506 Easter Slaughter of Jews and the Inquisition's *autos-da-fé*, events so horrific that it's now almost impossible to understand how thousands of ordinary people, not just a handful of madmen, could take part — and all in the name of religion. However, we didn't see a single marker or sign acknowledging these events.

This downplaying of the uncomfortable parts of history isn't confined to the Portuguese, I should add. We found much the same when we visited Tasmania where the Aboriginal genocide wasn't ignored but not exactly foregrounded. This could well be explained by the historical record being simply too scanty to provide a detailed account of what happened, though that's not the case with Portugal.

But there could be a bit more to this phenomenon than the existence of historical records, scanty or otherwise. Tasmania's convict history, for example, abounds in historical evidence and these former penal institutions with their miserable stone dormitories and dark solitary cells have become something of a tourist drawcard. So why is it that sites of convict brutality have become a tourist attraction but indigenous genocide has been treated more quietly?

Perhaps the reason for stories like the appalling treatment inflicted on native populations in America and Tasmania being somewhat minimized isn't so much to do with horror but rather something subtler — shame. As citizens of a country where such atrocities occurred and where so many of our forebears were to blame, avoidance is simply the least painful way of dealing with this reality.

But with events such as the transportation of convicts, there really isn't the same shame factor. The blame for this doesn't fall on a whole people but rather a much smaller group at the top of the social pile. We can't blame *ourselves* for the horrors of the penal system and under which, possibly, our forebears too might have suffered. It was the fault of the government and the men who were put in charge! With no shame involved, there's no need to suppress the stories and so they can be exposed to the healing light of day — and bring in the tourist dollar.

It's understandable why much of Portuguese — and Australian — history makes for uncomfortable reflection when you consider the massacring of native peoples, the floggings, burnings at the stake and so on. However, everyone we met in Portugal was friendly, helpful and knowledgeable. And though seeming somewhat selective when it came to remembering the past, they showed an excellent grasp of current affairs, with Portugal's high unemployment rate being of particular concern.

All in all, we loved the cheerful spirit of Lisbon with its cobbled streets winding up the hills, its lived-in but youthful vibe and the ever-present Tagus. I'd even go so far as saying I could happily live there — if I could only master the language, which isn't likely.

Sadly after a couple of fine days, it started pouring again. We'd moved on to one of Portugal's beautiful pousadas, the Castelo Óbidos, where it was an adventure just trying to find the castle gates, let alone negotiate the incredibly narrow winding lanes to the top. But once there it was magical with amazing views from the castle walls, delicious wine and reasonable food.

One helpful staff member tipped us off about the strangest and most un-Portuguese place we've ever visited — Buddha Eden. It had only recently opened so the fact that it wasn't yet well known, along with the bucketing rain, made for a very quiet, uncrowded visit. Although described as a garden, it was really more of a huge park. It had once been a farm but the owner, distraught after the Taliban's dynamiting of Afghanistan's stone Buddhas, decided to transform his land by creating a place dedicated to Buddhist sculptures, statues, pagodas and gardens.

It did seem a bit of an Eastern free-for-all as far as Buddhist art went with Buddhas of every kind — Chinese, Japanese, Thai — fat and laughing, elegantly reclining and everything in between. There was also a goodly assortment of Chinese dragons, Indian multi-armed deities and strangely, a life-sized replica of China's Terracotta Army. To top it off there was an impressive collection of contemporary works that might, with a bit of imagination, have some connection to Buddhism. But all this just added to the fun. It was a great day out, despite the deluge, definitely earning a big tick in the 'unexpected Portuguese experiences' box.

Another big tick went to a well-patronised café in Coimbra, the hilltop university town north of Lisbon where, much to our amusement, we were served two large glasses of port instead of the two coffees I thought I'd ordered. But even though it was only mid-morning, the waiter didn't miss a beat. Back in the UK, this order would have at least raised a merry joke but here, not so much as a subtle smirk. So much for my attempts at speaking Portuguese. Not wanting to admit my linguistic incompetence, we tried acting is if quaffing goblets of fortified wine at morning-tea time was perfectly normal, drank up and carried on.

No, I was decades too late to make Portugal my dream home. I loved it, I'd definitely go back but no way would I ever be able to conquer the lingo. So it was time to leave this dramatic land with its lashing rains and monster waves, Buddha Edens and horrible fiery histories and return to the softness of damp, grey England where sadly, I'd never be offered port — or heavenly custard tarts — for elevenses.

PET SITTING
NOVICES

5. Horse Country

Our two-month house swap in Goring-upon-Thames had gone so smoothly that soon after returning home we felt ready to embark on a longer and possibly riskier venture.

Energised from having just retired, we decided to take a 'senior gap year' — or two. The idea was to rent a furnished place somewhere in the UK. Now that we didn't have to be near London for work we could choose any place that took our fancy but the logistics of doing this would be scarily complicated, as we well knew from past experience. First we'd have to find someone we trusted to move into our place. Then we'd need to organise a car in the UK and find some cheap accommodation while we looked for something to rent within our limited budget. And that, we also knew from past experience, wouldn't be easy.

A house-sitting website was suggested by a friend, one who'd never actually tried it herself, so it was something of a gamble with no role model to give advice on what to look for or more crucially, avoid. But we eventually learned — the hard way.

Arranging our first pet sit happened incredibly quickly. Within minutes of finding what looked like a contender in Berkshire, a part of England we knew quite well, and typing my application, a positive response came straight back.

You never know what will be the one thing that particularly clicks with the person who's trying to find a sitter. In this case it was schools. In my application I'd mentioned to the poster, Sally, that we'd lived in the area a few years ago and I'd taught at a school that coincidentally turned out to be one where Sally's sons had competed in sporting events. Finding this sort of common ground isn't something you can plan but it definitely helps. Since house sitting and swapping are really all about trust, anything that helps forge a personal connection is a huge plus.

A follow-up Skype call went well so we had our first date in the diary. The house looked interesting — a large country estate with lovely gardens, a chicken coop, a small orchard and an on-site livery business. Our job would be to look after three dogs, two at night and three during the day, and feed the chickens and fish.

It was clear though, that the three weeks of this first assignment wouldn't be long enough to both buy a car and find a rental property so I set about finding one more. This proved trickier because the first time slot limited possible dates for the next. But as luck would have it, I soon found a dog sit advertised in a village not far from Oxford, well within our anticipated search area.

This time it wasn't common ground that sealed the deal but our willingness to live with the colour red. From the photos we could see that every room was either red or some other vibrant hue, which was obviously loved by the owners but could, as they themselves readily admitted, be a bit of a turn-off for less artistically adventurous souls. They had a point but they seemed such a nice couple, the dogs looked so appealing, the timing was spot on, as was the area, that I'd soon organised this as assignment number two. That would give us a few rent-free weeks to buy a car and start our house hunt.

So with friends organised to move into our place while we were away, our first pet sits and hire car lined up, we were set to go.

We arrived at the first property on a frosty morning before the owners left for their cruise. Having an hour or so to learn the ropes is very useful but a word of warning: Ensure there's a paper back up. As we've since discovered, it's hard to remember a lot of instructions delivered in one hit. Sally had helpfully written everything down so this wasn't a problem, although it did prove a headache on a later sit with a frantic dog-walking tour delivered at breakneck speed on a drive around the nearby countryside, with the result that all was rapidly forgotten and our dog charge got to know his own road and garden very well indeed.

Another word of warning: Beware unexpected animal sleeping arrangements. When Sally showed us our bedroom, I noticed that nestled near the bathroom door was a sweet little igloo dog bed. This, Sally told us, was where Smudge, the Jack Russell, would sleep. The others would stay downstairs in the utility room but Smudge expected human company at night. She would stay in her bed until we got up, Sally assured us, so we needn't worry about being disturbed. As we'd never shared a bedroom with an animal of any kind before we were surprised but not overly concerned. Just one more new experience!

Once left to our own devices, we unloaded the car and started to explore. The house was handsome, huge and sprawling with lots of additions from past renovations. I got lost trying to find the family bedroom when putting away Sally's last-minute laundry load, with so many levels and stairways, rooms leading to other rooms, doors opening onto corridors I hadn't realised were there, beautifully appointed sitting rooms, a vast dining room decorated with dozens of silver-framed family photos and, to literally top it off, a couple of lodgers' quarters under the eaves. Fortunately that was the only time I needed to venture beyond the main living areas so I didn't have to organise a basket of breadcrumbs to help me find my way back.

Even our wing was a bit complicated with a couple of adjoining bedrooms, shared bathroom and stairway to the downstairs utility/mud room where the dogs hung out when it was raining, which was most of the time. This room had doors to the garden, kitchen, eating nook and a little TV snug. It was interesting that the main living areas were relatively small compared to all those vast reception rooms but they were cosy, comfortable and the hub of the house throughout our stay.

We soon met the two lodgers who lived there during the week to be close to work and we enjoyed many a jolly evening together, perched on kitchen stools, while they cooked or did their laundry. Closer to weekends, it was a bit like party-time. Having lodgers around turned out to be an unexpected bonus.

Our regime was as follows: Richard would get up at dawn, rug up in his dressing gown and take the dogs out for a pee. Once it got a bit lighter and we were appropriately attired, we'd do a round of the grounds to feed the fish in the pond and let the chickens out of their coop. Then we'd sit up at the kitchen counter for a breakfast of fresh soft-boiled eggs while we checked used-car sites online. Our hire car was costing a small fortune so we needed to buy our own — and fast.

The house was set amidst horse paddocks and across the lane were acres of woodland so that's where we headed, twice a day, to walk the dogs. With the rutted muddy paths, ditches and ponds, this was quite a messy affair for humans as well as dogs. The weather was mostly sunny though with crisp frosty mornings, great for walking over mud. Hard, crunchy mud is much easier to negotiate than sodden, horse-pooey mud. It's much easier to appreciate the rationale for all that Roman road building once you've experienced trying to get over and around muddy, churned-up, brambly pathways.

It could also be a bit hairy at times too, as the woodland was popular with other dog walkers as well as horse riders. The nearby fields were just as muddy but were home to herds of cows, along with loads of cowpats, and rushing streams. The Jack Russells were very excited by all these other dogs, as well as the horses and cows, which led to many a rescue effort but also good opportunities for meeting some locals as we had a chat while struggling to keep our charges at bay. Our biggest but most endearing charge, a golden Labrador called Smidge, wasn't so interested in other animals but more keen on exploring thorny thickets and taking dips in the muddy ponds, which was all a bit messy but at least didn't involve potential bloodshed.

After the walk, we'd go through the routine of hosing mud off the dogs' feet in the stable yard and scraping the mud from our wellies, before heading off to look around car sales yards and do some food shopping. Then it was back for the dogs' afternoon walk with more shouting and leash tugging and a final round of mud scraping, dog scrubbing and chicken retrieval before sitting down to dinner with a much-needed glass of wine.

Finally we'd settle into an evening in the snug with the dogs. Smidge, the gentle Lab, was happy on her cushion but the more assertive Smudge was clearly accustomed to sharing the one small sofa with its human occupants. This dogs-on-furniture thing wasn't really a problem at first but after a few pet sits it did start to become something of an annoyance, especially in confined spaces.

So after a final trip out to the orchard for the dogs, with an occasional sighting of prowling foxes or wandering deer, it was up to our room with Smudge in tow. Now the story was that she was supposed to stay in her bed all night, which she did, at least at the start. But on the second morning when I woke up in the semi-dark, I noticed a dark slug-shaped blob near the bathroom door that seemed to slither along as I watched. Yes, it was Smudge — out of her bed and trying to unobtrusively make her way across the bedroom floor. At least she was quiet and didn't jump up on us. Not that day anyway.

Emboldened by her initial success, every morning after that she'd wake at first light and dropping any pretence of being inconspicuous, would simply bound out of her bed and jump up on whoever made eye contact first. It was all over then. No extra few minutes of sleep before facing the frosty orchard with all the pulling on of coats, hats and wellies to face the morning chores all over again. It was dog time — *now*!

At least we didn't have to deal with the horses. We quickly developed a deep respect for the two hardy young women who'd turn up at dawn each day to start their morning's work of hay forking, stall cleaning, and horse management. We just had the dogs, fish and chickens to worry about. Apart from the fish that barely counted, the chickens were the easiest. All we had to do was collect their eggs each morning and occasionally put new straw in the nesting boxes. Once let out of the coop they just roamed around the garden, orchard and stables all day. Then around dusk they'd appear out of nowhere, following us about like dogs until we opened their coop door and they'd happily head back in for the night.

Unfortunately, a couple of weeks later we had an unexpected and upsetting intrusion upon our country idyll. Without warning, Sally and James's three adult children descended upon us, along with baby and extra dog, because of a family crisis. Suddenly we found ourselves no longer master and mistress of a sprawling estate with the run of the snug and kitchen — the main wing with all its cavernous rooms being more or less out of bounds, not to mention freezing — but relegated, like hired help, to our upstairs quarters.

The family members, who'd arrived to provide moral support for the crisis-sufferer, took the opportunity to have an impromptu family reunion at the same time, taking over what had been our private domain. Now they were cooking meals, setting up high chairs, playing games in the dining nook, watching TV in the snug — all very jolly and rowdy, in spite of the crisis, but also very awkward for us.

The two lodgers weren't particularly affected as they had their own private sitting rooms but for us there was nowhere to go apart from our bedroom.

To add insult to injury, the oldest son, who lived nearby in what we assumed was a perfectly acceptable house for them to all hang out in, landed us with his dog to take on walks along with our agreed three, making dog walking from then on something of an exercise in resentment as we stomped along the muddy paths, struggling with the four dogs and stewing over his pomposity. He apparently considered house sitters as lowly beings who'd be perfectly happy being confined to quarters and looking after an extra dog. The unexpected interlopers had definitely put my Max nature's nose — or rather bill — out of joint. I missed 'my' home!

Seriously though, the whole principle of house sitting is based on reciprocity. It must be a win-win for both parties or it doesn't work. As their part of the bargain, house sitters provide services such as pet sitting, mail collection and plant watering. It's hard to put an exact monetary figure on this but a fair arrangement would be roughly two or three hours 'work' a day along with maintaining a 'lived-in' presence. In return, they expect to enjoy the privacy of a self-contained home, be it apartment, house or even château. Yes, we can include one of those in our catalogue of house-sitting pads.

Although sorely tempted to pack up and move on, we gritted our teeth and stuck it out until Sally and James returned. They were as shocked as we were to find a full house and couldn't apologise enough, though we never did reveal the bit about our upstairs banishment. From the point of view of 'trying lives' though, we learned something quite valuable. We lived the 'upstairs, downstairs' experience from both perspectives — first as the landed gentry at the top of the heap and then as the hired help at the bottom. There's nothing like a real-life experience to develop empathy and understanding.

So we departed in our newly acquired car, with mixed feelings and a final basket of fresh eggs, from what had essentially been a novel and enjoyable experience living as country squires in the home of this generous and courteous couple.

Having a few free days before moving on to our next pet sit and sorely in need of a spot of solitude but still quite enamoured of horses, we decided to stay in a converted stable within hiking distance of our beloved Daylesford Farm Shop. Three days of rest and relaxation awaited us. With delicious food from the farm shop and now unencumbered by dog walking, we'd have time to check out some of the rental properties we'd seen online.

The Stables had been accurately advertised as a 'Cotswold equine hideaway'. In fact it was so hidden away that after an hour's drive through the Chilterns in the pouring rain, the GPS took us to a place that definitely didn't look anything remotely like the photos on the website.

This wasn't a great start to our much anticipated relaxing break, with Richard in a temper at having to wedge the car precariously on the verge of a narrow muddy lane in fear of being rammed by tractors while I battled the elements running about looking for a road sign. No such luck! But a kindly lady opened her kitchen window and taking pity on me, shouted out a set of excellent directions: Drive a few metres back the way you came, past a wood and a big house and then down a long lane until you see a sign for Durham's Farm Riding School.

It was growing dark, ever colder and blowing a gale so we breathed a huge sigh of relief when the sign loomed into view. Our relief, however, was short-lived. At the end of the long drive we found ourselves amongst an assortment of seemingly abandoned buildings, barns, chicken coops, duck ponds, barking dogs, stables and horses with not a human in sight. Once again I ran about in the rain, Richard glowering in the car, until finally I heard human voices. Two young girls who cared for the horses were expecting us. They finished ministering to an agitated horse and then showed us the rickety stairs that led up to our equine attic hideaway. Fears of a possible *Cold Comfort Farm* experience momentarily gripped me. I doubted if our marriage would survive that level of rough farmyard squalor.

Much to my relief, it was quite the opposite. We found ourselves installed in a warm, cosy apartment and thanks to Daylesford Farm Shop where we'd stopped earlier that afternoon, managed to put together a picnic supper. We'd practically broken the bank for a container of organic kale and beetroot salad but with the rain, chicken poo, manure and mud, we'd run out of options since the nearest pub was closed for renovations. But we weren't grumbling. We had ample food and wine, and had landed, eventually, in this snug oasis. Max was happy.

After a good night's sleep and surprisingly missing Smudge and Smidge, we polished off a couple of our ladies' eggs and headed out on a perfect early spring

Cotswold morning. We soaked in the soft mist, blue skies, pale yellow primroses and snowdrops in the velvety grass verges — and breathed in contentment. If there was any such thing as a good life, at that moment, we were living it. And even better was to come because we had planned to spend the day in good company.

Later that morning we met up with friends, Avis and Peter, at Daylesford where we had fun checking out the exquisitely displayed produce, splurging on lunch in the café and buying some damson jam. Then it was a brisk country walk, minus dogs, and back to the Stables for tea, homemade scones and lemon drizzle cake, courtesy of Avis, before they drove back into more rain and the Big Smoke.

As for us, we spent another peaceful night with only a few rats scuttling in the roof and then country-style silence. We awoke to another freezing misty morning, rested and ready to leave horse country behind and set off for our next pet-sitting assignment in the Oxfordshire village of Brill.

6. Blown Away by Brill

Brill was an unusual village atop an extremely windy hill — complete with windmill. Its crazy landscape was gouged with holes from old pottery quarries but was now inhabited by the village cow herd and covered in heaps of dog and cow poo.

Jenny and Mike, the owners, were warmly welcoming, as were all the villagers we met during our stay. Jenny had placed fresh flowers on the dining table, a loaf of bread and some milk in the larder, and a list of useful information with handy phone numbers on the coffee table.

The little stone terrace cottage was a complete change from the estate we'd just come from, with its traditional pastel floral furnishings and expansive rooms filled with silver-framed family, dog and horse photos. Our Brill hosts were certainly not such conventional types but rather artistic, jazz-loving, free spirits.

Their cottage reminded me of Dawn French's vicarage in the TV series, *The Vicar of Dibley*, with similarly vivid red and blue walls, dark beams, decorative stars and moons, and a theatrical velvet sofa. The two upstairs bedrooms were painted a rich turquoise with more moons, starfish, shells and tiny jewel-coloured perfume bottles lining the bathroom shelves.

There was even a ghost. Well, at least the brief possibility of one. On our first morning there, I was checking my lipstick in the bedroom mirror when suddenly, behind my shoulder, appeared a glaring and glowering bearded face.

Heart pounding, I turned to find it was just a self-portrait of Mike on the wall directly behind me. The house was filled with many such realistic, life-size portraits of all kinds of characters, some of them quite scary looking, so I guess the shock could have been a lot worse.

Our charges this time were just two dogs, Red and Danni. Red was a huge, shaggy, well-behaved rescue dog of indeterminate breed while Danni was a smaller but surprisingly assertive Staffordshire terrier. We'd already dropped by the previous week so knew about their feeding routines, which were a bit tricky because of poor Red's dodgy intestinal tract, as well as good spots for walks.

Red was quite self-contained, happily taking himself off to his bed in the kitchen at night. But Danni, who was strangely very keen on the company of women, followed me everywhere: up and down the stairs, into the bathroom and into the bedroom where she had her own bed in the corner, just like Smudge. Thankfully though, unlike Smudge, Danni wasn't so keen on rising at the crack of dawn so stayed put until called to get up, which she'd do very reluctantly.

Although Red did have his basket in the kitchen, taking up almost half the space because of his immense size, we soon discovered that we needed to close the kitchen door before heading up to bed ourselves. Already a bit shaken from seeing that glowering face looming behind me, I had another shock when I got up in the dead of night only to step straight onto a soft, warm, shaggy body — a living, breathing bedside rug. It was Red, who must have woken during the night and spying the open kitchen door, had quietly loped upstairs to join the gang. After that literally hairy experience, the kitchen door was firmly closed at bedtime.

Our daily routine began once again with long-suffering Richard getting up in the cold, rugging up in his dressing gown and taking the dogs out for a short comfort break. After breakfast we'd take them for their first long walk around the village or if the weather was reasonable, a bit further afield in Jenny's car.

As we were in the throes of full-on house hunting, which was become ever more worrying as the weeks passed without us having found anything suitable, we'd then usually head out for a few hours to look at properties. One problem with the cottage was that there was no dog flap or outside shed, which meant the dogs had to stay indoors whenever we went out. Worried about leaving them for more than a few hours, we could only look at one or two properties a day and this dragged the whole process out far longer than we'd hoped. Rushing back in the late afternoon, we'd arrive home to see two expectant faces at the window, eagerly awaiting their last long walk, which was followed by dinner — both dog and human.

There were two sofas in the red sitting room. The dark blue velvet sofa was ours and the black leather one was for the dogs. They obeyed this rule pretty well, so on this sit we weren't all squashed together on one sofa and constantly covered in dog hair. At around nine Red would lope off to his giant bed in the kitchen while Danni hung out with us until we made our move, at which point she'd race upstairs ahead of us, nearly knocking me sideways no matter how hard I tried to beat her to it. There was no way she'd miss out on joining her bedroom companions.

When we first arrived we were concerned that our three-week stint might be a bit of a stretch. The village wasn't all that big and the walks not particularly pleasant, what with all those pock-marked hillocks, cowpats and blasting winds, but those misgivings were soon dispelled, thanks to Richard losing the house keys.

It was our second morning in Brill. We headed out into the blustery cold for the dogs' first walk of the day, only to find on our return that the bunch of house and car keys was no longer in Richard's pocket. In between locking the door, hanging onto big Red, restraining Danni from rushing off to eat dog poo (her favourite treat), rummaging with poo bags and coping with our thick gloves, the keys had somehow escaped.

What to do? Through the cottage window we could see, invitingly, our phones, the warm sitting room and Jenny's list of handy phone numbers. We had no money, no contact details and no phone to call anyone even if we did. So backtracking with the two bewildered dogs, we searched every leaf-sodden, muddy path, trying to find them. With no luck there, we began clutching at straws.

Across the road from the cottage was the general store where we might at least take refuge for a bit while we regrouped and figured out what to do. Once we explained our plight, the very helpful manager seemed perfectly happy acting as the point of contact between us and any potential key finders. In a village like Brill, expecting someone to turn in a bunch of lost keys didn't seem at all crazy and the general store did seem, after all, the most sensible place to do just that, being the only shop in town and something of a social hub.

We couldn't hang about in there indefinitely so once again we braved the elements, with me huddling with the dogs in our temporarily absent neighbours' doorway while Richard backtracked again and again trying to find those wretched keys. Poor Danni and Red were shivering but in good spirits, though I was wondering how long my two sodden tissues would last in all that cold. I was wondering too — as I was starting to feel a bit desperate — if in my unkempt, bedraggled state, I'd be bold enough to brazen my way into the rather posh Pointer's Pub loo.

However, while I was huddled in the doorway with the dogs, Richard was not just investigating but also making friends. While searching on the village green, he fell into conversation with a delightful couple who, after sympathizing about the lost house keys, practically forced Richard into joining the church choir — the ranks of which were apparently somewhat depleted — in time to sing in the coming Easter service.

Since we were not exactly churchgoers, this seemed a good excuse not to join. But no, they assured him. This wouldn't be a problem at all. In fact practically the entire church community was more or less of the same inclination. It was the community part — and the music — that was the point.

But getting the ball rolling and actually joining the choir proved to be just slightly tricky as it entailed contacting the choirmaster. Even though word of mouth worked extremely well in this somewhat quirky community, other forms of communication left a lot to be desired. It turned out that because phone connectivity in

Brill was so poor, we'd only be able to communicate with the choirmaster by phone when we called from *his* kitchen, which sort of defeated the whole purpose of calling. Perhaps it would have been easier to leave him a note at the general store.

We never did get to the bottom of this strange communication problem and Richard didn't end up joining the choir, which might have been a mistake in retrospect. Turning down an opportunity to be part of a new community isn't something we usually do, but we had other fish to fry right then — finding somewhere to live post-Brill. However, we did at that point begin to feel part of the village. Even losing keys can have a silver lining.

Eventually, thanks to the return of our knowledgeable next-door neighbours, we were able to contact Jenny's daughter who lived in the next village and had a spare set of keys. And thanks to the lost keys we celebrated another silver lining — meeting these neighbours who, despite our miserable situation and looking like something the cat had dragged in, invited us for drinks and nibbles that evening. So, more friends in Brill and now every reason to look forward to the next three weeks.

An hour later we were rescued and back in the cottage. Warmth, loo, water, tissues! But even though we were safely inside, the keys were still missing. All that night we were gripped by the nagging fear of robbers finding the keys, breaking in, cleaning out the house that wasn't even ours, and driving off in Jenny's car.

But on Sunday morning, still despondent and depressed, we heard a knock at the door. A lady standing on the doorstep tentatively asked if we'd lost any keys. She'd found a set down the road the day before and noticed the car key on the fob was for a Subaru and today she'd seen a Subaru parked outside. Was it ours? Richard hugged her and invited her for a drink at the Pointer or Pheasant (Brill's only two pubs) next time we met. Such sweet relief! New friends, keys found and nights when we could sleep easy, unworried about waking up to find Jenny's car had been driven off by car thieves.

As I've just mentioned, Brill had two pubs, the Pheasant and the slightly trendier Pointer. We patronized both but for village gossip and bonhomie we'd head to the Pheasant, which was more of a casual hangout. It was here that a group of very friendly drinkers gave us a fascinating insight into village genealogy by informing us, with perfectly straight faces, that all the locals were inbred. We ran that claim by some other locals, or people we thought of as locals, and they all totally agreed. However, on further probing it turned out that hardly anyone we met actually *was* a local, at least in terms of going back generations. So who all those inbred villagers actually were remains a mystery to this day. But this much *was* clear — that camaraderie, a love of story telling and a sense of humour were alive and well in Brill.

It was at the Pheasant too, that we were given the low-down on the most famous local, Tony Blair. At least we didn't have to wonder if he was one of the infamous inbreds, since he was Scottish. But he was certainly considered infamous because of his decision to join George Bush in the invasion of Iraq — roundly criticized by all — as well as being the owner of many mansions and stately homes, including one in the nearby village of Underwood.

One lady told me about an evening at the pub when someone tried to squeeze beside her on the long settle. As she moved over to make room, she realized it was Cherie Blair with Tony following close behind. Others at the table had to restrain the lady's husband, furious about the Iraq war, from 'landing one' on Tony. No, it wasn't all peace and love in Brill — not when it came to the Iraq debacle, the Blairs, and them living it up in their walled mansion complete with woods and lakes.

We already knew they lived in the area because on our earlier visit Jenny had driven us to Wotton Lakes, where the Blair house is located, to show us some dog-walking trails. Being a private estate with restricted entrances and multiple security cameras, only a few passes were in circulation but luckily for us, Jenny had one.

Walking the dogs around the lakes was the highlight of our three weeks in Brill, with their woods, ducks and spring flowers budding in the mossy grass. We never did run into the Blairs, which might have been for the best, but we did meet a few anglers and fellow dog walkers who were delighted to share tales of any rare sightings. As we learned from our stay there, Tony Blair will be remembered, not so much for 'Cool Britannia' but for 'Sack Iraq.'

Brill is most famous though for its windmill. We could see that it was picturesque but its more practical function wasn't so obvious until it started to really blow a gale. Windmills are of course erected where there's *wind* so it shouldn't have been such a surprise to find that our daily walks on Brill Common were unfailingly awfully windy and during really bad weather, eye-wateringly windy. Although now static, it was clear from the hillside, pockmarked from centuries of clay digging and brick making, and from the grazing cattle and fertile fields beyond, that the windmill must have been an invaluable energy source for Brill's earlier inhabitants.

We spent a couple of days with family and friends sharing Brill's attractions — well, its one attraction, the windmill — and allowing them to experience Mother Nature in full force — not only the roaring winds but also bucketing rain, hail, the ubiquitous mud and the cold. Later, while ploughing through the mud around Wotton Lakes, clutching hats, caps and dogs with grim determination, we gratefully took refuge in handily located gazebos and whimsical follies, or if too far from any of these, huddled under rhododendron bushes.

For the total pain/pleasure experience, so popular with the 'mustn't grumble' Brits, we would end these bracing walks in the warmth and relative calm of the Pointer's snug or the Pheasant's fireplace bar. And yes, of course we'd tuck into some wonderful roast beef with Yorkshire pudding followed by steamed ginger pudding and custard.

We'd been spending countless hours scouring real estate websites and driving from one county to another in search of habitable and affordable accommodation. We soon knew to be wary of any property that had photos of little more than an artfully placed antique chest on what looked like a spacious landing and a close-up of an attractive wood-burning fire place. The reality was usually a poky bedroom under the eaves, no hanging space, ugly carpet, a kitchen out of the '50s and a miserable downstairs bathroom wedged behind the kitchen.

We quickly realized that our original plan of renting a furnished property was totally unrealistic. Years ago it was the norm for rental properties to be fully furnished and judging from our experience at that time, the furnishings were generally of good quality. Now the opposite was true. Perhaps it was because there were now so many short-term holiday lets on the market. High-turnover properties rarely boast quality décor but are furnished to withstand plenty of wear and tear. But even so, it's much cheaper and less complicated for landlords to let out their properties unfurnished. So we narrowed our search to unfurnished properties only, which meant we needed something small and not too expensive to furnish ourselves.

One apartment seemed to be spot on. It was just the right size and in an area we liked, the spa town of Cheltenham in Gloucestershire. Our good friend Pamela lived in the building so we already knew it to be a well-designed, modern complex with spacious balconies looking out over communal gardens. Although at the top of our price range, we thought it would be worth it.

Pamela had arranged an inspection so we'd booked a table at her favourite restaurant, the Daffodil, expecting soon to be celebrating the signing of the lease. What greeted us at the apartment though, was an absolute disaster zone. As far as the layout and space went, the apartment was absolutely fine. But the mess! The current tenant, who was out at the time, was the daughter of a Russian oligarch. If we'd thought the adult children at our first horse country dog sit were somewhat entitled, this took entitlement to a whole different level.

I've never seen such disregard for one's own and other people's property. Clothes, including her knickers, were strewn over the floor and on every surface of every room. This young lady knew the estate agent was bringing people around, which was even more astonishing. And it wasn't just clothes that were strewn about but also dirty dishes, half-empty glasses, overflowing ashtrays, chewed chop bones, pizza boxes, makeup — and I haven't even mentioned the bathroom! The poor, shocked agent tried to assure us that the place would be thoroughly cleaned before we moved in but by then we'd totally lost our enthusiasm so retreated to the Daffodil, not to celebrate but to commiserate.

Eventually though, we did find two contenders and needed to decide between them — and fast.

One, the Clock Tower, was in Broxwood near Hereford on the Welsh borders. This is another area we loved, being a bit further from Cheltenham but close to Hay on Wye in Wales, and surrounded by beautiful wooded countryside. It looked good on the website but after so many bad experiences we knew not to get our hopes up from the photos alone. However, it actually turned out to be something very special.

The flat itself, which was quite spacious, was above the gateway through which coaches would have driven years ago. But it was the grounds that enchanted us. They were spectacular with peacocks, chickens, vegetable gardens, sculptured hedges and views to die for — secluded but totally idiosyncratic in a Harry Potter kind of way.

The owners were pleasantly quirky, a trait we've grown to appreciate more and more, and regaled us with tales of hunt balls where scandalous goings-on in the pool once left them with a barrel full of discarded undies to deal with. (They burned them.)

We fell in love with it. We had visions of dinner parties with our other neighbours who would surely be equally as interesting — there were at least three other flats in various parts of the property — as well as wonderful walks in the woodlands, attending the Hay on Wye literature festival and visiting the local black and white villages.

However, we'd also seen another property, a small two-up, two-down stone cottage in Chipping Campden that was also a strong contender. Actually, the *only* other contender because after eliminating scores from our search, these two were the only ones we could both afford and where we could contemplate living.

The Chipping Campden cottage was tiny but light-filled and in a beautiful Cotswold village but it seemed a bit boring compared to the whimsical Clock Tower. It had one advantage though, in that it wouldn't be available for a few weeks as the owner was redecorating. This suited us very well indeed as we'd agreed to a house sit in France and didn't want to let the owners down by cancelling at the last minute.

We couldn't make up our minds. We agonized, asked advice, and then did a sensible cost/benefit analysis, which was very revealing.

It was Oxford that swung it. We'd just had a day's break from house hunting in Oxford, which was within striking distance of the Cotswolds and that now had to be taken into account. Would it be better being close to Hereford's cathedral or Oxford's colleges? Oxford's (and Stratford upon Avon's) theatres or Hay on Wye's Literature Festival? Leominster's somewhat dull

Morrison's supermarket or Oxford's more glamorous Waitrose? The Harry Potter-like Clock Tower in Broxwood or Tolkien's local pub, the Eagle and Child, in Oxford?

So Oxford was the decider. Our potential future eccentric Clock Tower life would now be unrealized and in spring we'd be moving into a bijou but more conventional residence in Chipping Campden.

Our time in Brill was drawing to a close and though excited about moving on to our next house sit, we were sad to be leaving Brill, especially after one final act of kindness by the manager of the general store. Our next sit in France was mostly going to entail home maintenance and redecorating so the owners had asked if we could accept delivery of some speciality wallpaper they'd ordered from a British company and bring it along with us.

That was fine but with us out house hunting for much of the time, it was proving hard to organize its delivery. The cottage opened directly onto the street and with no rear access there was nowhere to leave packages. However, the owner of the general store once again came to our rescue, being perfectly happy to keep a lookout and take delivery of any rolls of wallpaper that might arrive on our doorstep.

So we left Brill with fond memories. Village life, we'd discovered, had many attractions. Our weeks in Brill had allowed us to be part of an England where the church still played a vital part in village life — though religious belief was optional — where pubs were a hive of communal activity, where you could walk to everything, and where everyone looked out for everyone else. People returned keys, village shopkeepers acted as go-betweens and neighbours asked you over for drinks or to join the church choir after only a day's acquaintance.

We were really hoping that our year in Chipping Campden would be as heartwarming as Brill — but not as bone-chillingly windy.

A YEAR IN
THE COUNTRY

7.   Quirky Cotswolds

The night before the start of our lease, we stayed overnight in nearby Broadway to be close at hand for moving into our cottage the next morning. This would be our home base for the next year — a quiet, non-eventful place (or so we thought) and being in the heart of England, handy for a few far-flung adventures.

First up was to collect the keys from the courteous and accommodating real estate agent — so accommodating that he had organised to be around to take delivery of our new bed a few days earlier so we would at least have somewhere to sleep when we moved in. Knowing we would be away for up to two years but expecting to rent a furnished property, we had only shipped clothes and a few other essentials — mainly books, computers and files — so we knew our first few days would be fairly Spartan. A bed though, was essential.

Next up was to get in some supplies and pack them away in the tiny, English-style fridge. Actually, it was a bar fridge but we managed perfectly well for the year, which goes to show that it's not hard to adjust one's shopping behaviour to fit the situation and save space and energy at the same time.

Finally it was time to explore our new village. As the cottages were terraced, we shared adjoining walls and garden fences with our neighbours, which made getting to know them quite easy. On one side was the local surgery's practice manager — a very helpful neighbour indeed — and on the other, a retired bachelor with an understandably timid rescue whippet that had been stabbed through the head by her previous owner and had lost an eye. Luckily she had found herself with a decent human being this time round, who was happy getting up early each morning to walk her round the village in the freezing pre-dawn mist. A labour of love indeed.

Soon afterwards we met the local councillor's wife who gave us the buzz on the mayor who moonlighted as Bobo the Clown, the friendly washing machine man who was just like everyone's Uncle Dave, the smartly dressed and bejewelled librarian, and the two informative ladies at the information centre who told us all about the *big event* taking place that very weekend. It seems we'd arrived just in time for the Cotswold Olimpicks, famed forerunner of the Olympic Games that we know and love today.

This fun and historic event was to kick off on Friday with the Scuttlebrook Races followed by the Wheelbarrow. (Bring your own barrows, so the posters instructed.) But the scary thing was that our removal company was set to deliver our goods and chattels that same day, just when the streets would be closed off to make way for all the incoming Olimpick fair vehicles — apparently an endless stream of trucks with funfair rides, snack stalls and marquees.

Happy days! I couldn't wait to see how many potential friends we'd alienate after tying up the whole village while the movers unloaded our stuff. It had also started pouring with rain — par for the course on moving day. Just our luck.

There wasn't anything to be done but hope for the best and look forward to what was to come. Unless we were run out of town beforehand, we couldn't wait for the shin-kicking, tug of war, and torchlight procession that were slated for later that night — though a little anxiety niggled as to whether a Wicker Man figured in these ancient festivities.

So much for expecting a dozy time in sleepy Chipping Campden.

The next morning the village gods smiled upon us. I'd risen on Friday morning to brewing storm clouds and headed to the library — our temporary connection to the world with its free Wi-Fi — in wind, rain and hail, fearing the worst. The moving van would arrive and block off the road outside for an hour; irate villagers would tar and feather us, or even worse, single us out for the Wicker Man celebration later that night; and the Olimpicks would be held in freezing rain.

Happily, none of that came to pass. Well, the freezing bit did but we were at least spared the rain. At the very moment that I was beavering away at the library computer, the movers had arrived and were delivering our boxes to a very much-relieved Richard — and neighbours. By the time I'd battled my way home through the hail, Richard had already unpacked half the boxes, neatly folded the wrapping paper and the sky was beginning to brighten, as were our spirits.

So after a busy afternoon trying to find places to put things, we were ready to carve a pathway through empty boxes, find the front door and head up Dover Hill to discover exactly what these Olimpicks were all about. Once at the top we discovered what turned out to be the best part of the whole event — a panoramic view west over the Cotswold foothills and valley beyond.

After that it was hard to decide between the camels or the birds of prey, the Amazing Star ride playing rock hits from the '50s or the Punch and Judy show, the marching band or the Morris dancers. Off to one side of the main activity area I noticed a high, suspicious-looking pole with a huge bale of straw stuck on top. Was it some sort of feeding apparatus for the camels? Or did it have a more sinister purpose? The *Wicker Man* is a movie not easily forgotten.

Down below, surrounded by a very steep, precarious kind of natural amphitheatre was a flattish piece of land for the games proper: the obstacle course, sack race, picture game (too complicated to even try to explain) and the pièce de résistance, the shin-kicking competition.

One can't expect perfection, so although the weather stayed fine and dry, the evening was far from mild. Not only was it bitterly cold up on that exposed hilltop but we also had to dodge mounds of soggy cowpats and other assorted animal droppings, which left our shoes in a horrible state. But hey, it was England, early spring, and we were in the countryside. A blasting gale and some mucky mud wasn't going to put off these hardy villagers so a good time was had by all in a typically grin-and-bear-it, mustn't-grumble English fashion.

As the energetic MC drew the festivities to a close, I finally discovered the actual function of that huge straw edifice. It was a kind of ancient torch to be lit at sunset as a fire source for the torchlight procession. Relief, once again.

The MC's final words really struck a chord. Announcing the commencement of the torchlight procession, he described how, on the road back to the village, we'd have the setting sun behind us and moon in front.

'My God, we live in a lovely place!' he exclaimed.

Indeed.

I have to make the painful admission that not being as hardy as the other villagers — one day hadn't really been long enough to become accustomed to the Arctic conditions of Dover's Hill — we bailed and headed to the pub, hoping to watch the tail end of the torchlight procession from the warmth of the Red Lion's snug. We'd had a minor disagreement as to which pub offered the better view — the Red Lion or the more upmarket Lygon Arms — but my choice, the Lion, had won out. Even Richard ultimately agreed that the state of our shoes might be frowned upon at the Arms and he wasn't keen on being turfed out on our first visit.

However, yet again, we failed to withstand the evening's many challenges. We found a good spot near a window looking out onto the square where the procession would end and where we could watch the band. What drove us out this time wasn't the Dover's Hill cold but the very rowdy mob sitting behind us whose idea of fun was to cheer each other on, very noisily, in seeing who could build the highest beer-glass tower. Shin kicking was one thing but this raucous competition was too much, so admitting defeat, we bailed yet again, this time for home and so totally missed the torchlight procession.

Maybe, we consoled ourselves, if we were still here next year we might have acclimatized enough to join in. But remembering how that torchlight procession in Goring ended up with me copping a singed jacket — maybe not.

Saturday's festivities, the oddly named Scuttlebrook Wake, were of a very different and more recognisable variety. I had no idea what it was actually all about but it seemed to be a combination of a primary school open day, May Day festivities and some kind of fancy dress and fancy float competition, with a whole bunch of truly tacky rides and side stalls to complete the fun.

What had once been a pristine, chocolate-box Cotswold village was now transformed into a fun fair with raucous, eye-wateringly lurid-coloured rides abutting the pale gold cobblestones and soft grey roofs.

The festivities began with the arrival and crowning of the new Scuttlebrook Queen, along with her attendants, all beautifully kitted out in romantic, floral outfits. Then the two local primary schools, one Anglican and one Catholic, came out onto the asphalt square to perform some folk-dancing routines, including some pretty fancy Maypole moves.

The black asphalt and the dances — though not the Maypole — brought back fond memories of similar events at my primary school in the '50s. Richard didn't have the same sense of déjà vu since folk dancing didn't figure in Florida's school curriculum. But I remembered the lively enjoyment, despite the boys' feigned protests, of dressing up in yellow wattle-sprigged outfits to perform before our parents on Education Day. It was unexpectedly heart-warming to experience the same sense of community that I had felt all those years ago and to realise how close still are the cultural bonds between Australia and Britain.

After the school kids came a lively round of Morris dancing; a group of brightly coloured, raggedy Mummers; a fancy dress competition and finally the arrival of the floats. These were meant to be humorous, quite a challenge as the theme was Chipping Campden in wartime. While watching all this I made friends with a lady wedged beside me. Actually I first noticed her when she pushed in front of me but I was also drawn to her rather lovely peach cashmere cardigan, very much in keeping with the spring festivities.

It turned out that she belonged to the Women's Institute (WI) and when she discovered I'd just moved into the village and wasn't 'just a tourist' she became very keen for me to join. Very keen. She clasped my hand, earnestly assuring me that she'd remember my name and ominously, where I lived.

There was even a WI float. Good grief! Maybe that would be me wearing the tight-perm wig and broad-shouldered '40s style suit next year, taking pride of place on the WI float. Maybe Richard would be prancing around with bells on his gaiters and waving white handkerchiefs with the Morris dancers! Or would the prospective fun and games of the Mummers prove more tempting? We'd nearly succumbed to joining the Brill church choir at Easter so it wasn't totally out of the question.

And if I *were* minded to join the WI, how long before I was barred? The peach cardigan-wearing lady was very clear that they had strong links to the church.

But with the sky once again darkening, a more pressing question arose. Would I ever wear summer clothes again?

Our honey-coloured stone cottage had two good-sized bedrooms and a bathroom upstairs and a small open-plan living room, kitchen and powder room downstairs. The second bedroom, which we used as a study, looked out over the little back garden and the church steeple beyond. Both bedrooms had built-in closets so this reduced our furniture spend. All we'd had to buy for the upstairs rooms was a bed, a couple of bedside tables and a table that could double as a desk.

The master bedroom was at the front and each morning we woke to a view of the orchard across the road, with its flock of sheep. It wasn't a busy road as far as cars were concerned but there was a fair amount of pedestrian traffic with tourists wandering by and peeking in our kitchen window, villagers heading to the doctors' surgery a few houses down and horses from the nearby stables clopping by. When we eventually moved out a year later, it was the 'cloppers' and the orchard we missed most and at times still do.

We took particular care to buy only what we'd be happy taking with us when we left. This meant buying stools, chairs and side tables that could be used inside but could also easily be carried outside on those rare sunny days when we hoped to sit in the courtyard. As the living room was also the dining area, we bought an inexpensive drop-leaf table that could be extended for guests, a sofa that would be perfect to replace our old one in Sydney and stackable chairs that are always handy anywhere. Ikea and charity shops were our chief ports of call for most items, so we were able to furnish our cottage at a moderate price.

It didn't take long to get comfortably settled and begin trying out our new lives as Chipping Campden villagers.

We soon found that Campden had a few fairly distinct groups, though these were by no means mutually exclusive and a certain amount of fluidity was accepted.

Firstly, there was the group characterized by the rowdy, beer-glass-tower-erecting lot from the pub. This group I pretty well avoided but somehow I doubt they would have been offended. They rarely, if at all, overlapped with any of the other groups.

Secondly, there were the cashmere cardigan-wearing ladies and checked shirt- and tie-wearing gentlemen who seemed to predominate in the village. They were to be found in everyday venues such as the butcher's, post office, library, churches and, if women, the WI. I found I could fit in quite well with this group, though it was a tad tiring after a few hours.

However, I did actually go to a WI meeting and much to my surprise, really enjoyed it. My first and enduring reaction was finding it to be cheerful, warm and life affirming. Being one of *them* wouldn't be bad at all. Happily there was no further mention of church but the WI's Scuttlebrook Wake float was mentioned as soon I checked in with the ladies who were welcoming guests at the door. I'd already been marked as a likely floatee, as I'd feared.

The ladies sold me raffle tickets with the three prizes being a large punnet of strawberries, a basket of asparagus and a bunch of roses, all at their peak just then. I didn't win, which was a shame as they all looked splendid. A lot more useful too, than the waterbed Richard had won a few years ago at his high school reunion in Florida. Amazingly it was the prize for coming the furthest distance. Heaven knows what they were thinking — or rather, not thinking. Certainly not about how we'd get it home on a trans-Pacific flight. Luckily he managed to swap it for a bottle of champagne.

Kathleen, she of the apricot cashmere cardigan, had dropped by *very early* a couple of days before to invite me to the meeting while I was in the garden hanging out some washing. This time she was dressed in a lovely bright citrus spotted sweater, while I looked very much like a paid-up member of Group One in housework clothes, wet hair and, I have to admit, the odd curler.

At least, I consoled myself as I stood at the door embarrassed at my unkempt state, I'd have plenty of time to prepare and make sure I was wearing the right gear. Something unobtrusive that would blend in. I was so grateful that my checked Jaeger skirt had arrived. I was going to have to make some pretty serious changes to my appearance if I wanted to avoid disgracing myself. The prospect of being shunned by these neatly dressed ladies and having to hang out at the Lion with a bunch of Group Ones building beer-glass towers on Saturday evenings, wasn't too appealing.

The third group was made up of walkers, instantly recognisable by their walking gear: hardwearing trousers, rugged jackets, heavy boots, backpacks and attractively carved sticks. We fitted in fine with this group, though we had to pretend we were more knowledgeable and more experienced country walkers than actually was the case.

For example, we'd bought a local walking map that Richard was relying on one day to take us from the trendy Meg Rivers café a couple of miles away back to Campden along the Heart of England Way. Somehow he got us off-piste and we ended up at the scarily named anaerobic digestion plant. We shuddered to think what it was but from the stench and all the danger signs around, we suspected — not good. Actually we later discovered that anaerobic digesters are great for reducing greenhouse gases by converting food waste to energy but at that time we were still innocents in such country ways.

After going in smelly circles up hill and down dale for about an hour, a welcome member of Group One — though obviously upwardly mobile and eventually headed for Group Two and whose pheasant farm we'd accidentally wandered onto — showed us the escape route down through the happily rose-scented village of Broad Campden to home.

The fourth and last group were the tourists. We had no desire to blend in with this group since we were now locals. How superior we could now feel as we confidently strode down the High Street knowing that we were among the blessed few who actually *lived* in this idyllic place that they were all so busily photographing.

We did briefly think we'd stumbled across a new, as yet unidentified group one morning as we drove through the nearby village of Blockley on one of our exploratory excursions. It was still quite early so we were surprised to see all kinds of people, young and old, out chatting in the street and on the pavement.

I was thinking how nice it was — a young workman chatting to an elderly lady dressed in a quaint pinafore — and so many villagers out this early. Lovely! It looked like the vintage car club was strong here too. And there was a young girl in a longish dress and cloak holding a posy. Charming! And there was someone with a clapperboard — and another with a walkie-talkie — and 'Closed Street' signs.

The penny dropped. No, we hadn't come across a sighting of what was possibly a new and rare fifth group at all. We were in the middle of a film shoot.

8. Summer's Sweet Excess

Eventually summer did arrive, along with towering hollyhocks growing from the most impossible nooks and crannies in cottage walls. We were now fully immersed in Cotswold village life. I had been embraced by the Women's Institute; we were on first-name basis at Campden's best coffee shop; we were regulars at the local greengrocer's which was well-stocked with local produce, sold by the handful — or paper bag; and we had our seniors' bus passes. We'd also joined the National Trust, the best investment we've ever made.

The monthly film club at the old Town Hall, like the WI, turned out to be another good opportunity to meet the locals. We always looked forward to a 'Flicks in the Sticks' evening. We'd start with a stroll down the High Street catching glimpses of different lives through the cottage windows, just as Alain de Botton had done in Amsterdam. It was fascinating to see antique furniture being used for everyday living rather than being treated as museum pieces. Warm wooden bookcases; the golden glow of lamps on polished tables; families playing pianos, preparing meals and sitting around chatting together — these lives seemed very inviting indeed.

Then we'd cut across the cobblestones of the ancient Market Hall to the Town Hall where we'd be treated to movies like *The Second Best Marigold Hotel* with a bunch of people who, us included, looked like potential Marigold Hotel residents themselves, with wine, beer and Group Two cheer aplenty.

Walking, as I said earlier, is the best way to get to know a place and this was certainly true of our year in Campden. Whether on a short stroll around the village or a more arduous trek over surrounding hills and fields, we'd always find ourselves chatting with someone we already knew or that we'd just met in passing. The hike over the steep hill to Broadway was one of our favourites. We'd walk the few miles there, have coffee and cake and then catch the bus back, the hill being steeper heading out of Broadway than heading in.

But my favourite was the shorter walk across the fields to Broad Campden. This is one aspect of life in the UK that we don't find in Australia or the US — the ability to roam across farmland, woodland and even, via defined routes, private property — as long as there's a legal footpath. Broad Campden had a great little pub, the Baker's Arms, lots of picture-perfect cottages and a Quaker meetinghouse where one day we noticed a sign offering tea and cake along with a talk on the history of the place. This turned out to be refreshing, not only to body but also to heart. They were such a gentle group of people who gave a short but fascinating account of their movement — I don't know if it could actually be called a church — in this very simple, mellow stone building.

I asked why it was that Quakerism hadn't flourished in the same way as other comparatively new religious groups had, for example, the Mormons in America? Money and power, was their short answer, though expressed without a hint of bitterness. That's the way of the world, they acknowledged. For a religious movement to grow, it must be backed by money and from money flows power: power of the press, political power and social power.

It's ironic, looking at the current political landscape in the US, that William Penn, the most well-known Quaker, being the founder of Pennsylvania, ended up as real estate developer. Does this sound familiar? Unfortunately, that's as far as any comparison with Donald Trump goes. Penn was imprisoned for fighting against the oppression of free speech; Trump attacks the press. Penn hated tyranny; Trump praises tyrants. Penn was compassionate; Trump is cruel. Penn was driven by the superego; Trump is all id.

Unfortunately though, Penn ended up in dire financial straits and was forced to return to England where his final resting place can be found in the Quaker graveyard at Jordans, a pretty wooded village in Buckinghamshire. Sadly Quakerism seems to be dwindling but meeting houses can still be found in most towns and cities, even in tiny villages like Broad Campden. If we were to become churchgoers, Richard and I would most likely seek out the nearest Quaker community.

It's interesting and perhaps paradoxical to consider how crucial money can be in the growth of a religion while at the same time it can lead to horrendous abuse if money and power take too strong a hold. Those Inquisitions in Europe and the enslaving of conquered peoples in the New World weren't just about rooting out heretics and oppressing freedom of speech and religion. There were also financial and property-grabbing motives. The political movers and shakers, both religious and secular, certainly knew how to manipulate mobs with their 'bread and circuses' rallies, public ritual humiliations, and stoking of anger and fear. Sounding even more familiar?

Again, it comes down to a balancing act — having enough money to get going but not to such excess that corruption takes over. It seems that the meek inherit the earth with great difficulty. This is one time when excess is *not* so sweet.

୬

Fortunately, our Cotswold village had managed to maintain this precarious balancing act very well. We were lucky enough to be in town during the annual Chipping Campden Literature Festival and what a treat it was. The theme that year was history — right up my alley.

We heard the charismatic Janina Ramirez talking about her recently published book, *Power, Passion and Politics in Anglo Saxon England: The Private Lives of the Saints*. Having majored in Early English, I was thrilled to relive some of those medieval texts written by monks in centuries past, working in their stone cloisters and libraries not so far from Chipping Campden.

Her talk was held in the centuries-old Town Hall that, along with Janina's enthusiasm, bold lacy black dress, dramatic eye shadow and bright red lipstick, created a highly charged yet mysterious atmosphere. I was inspired all over again and lapsed briefly into regret that I hadn't pursued even more advanced studies and landed an exciting academic and broadcasting career — just as she had done! But wistfully pushing thoughts of unfulfilled ambitions aside, I lined up to buy the book.

Next up was David Wilkinson, with a PhD in both astrophysics and theology, to discuss his book, *When I Pray, What Does God Do?* This time the location was another of Campden's listed buildings, St James' Church, a location well befitting the subject matter.

We were sitting in the front pew beside the author while he waited to be introduced so we chatted a bit before his talk started. I decided to be upfront, telling him we weren't believers but were very interested in hearing what he had to say. He was gently sympathetic while making a valiant effort not to be judgmental. His talk though, turned out to be quite thought provoking and brought to mind those medieval saints and later inquisitors who were the exact opposite. There was no freedom to question or disagree in those groupthink times. Not much at Trump rallies either, come to think of it.

My ears really perked up when he started talking about strange stuff in the Cosmos: quantum physics, chaos theory, string theory and how God might exist within — or without — space-time. Intriguing! But in question time when I asked him to define God he reverted, much to my disappointment, to all the usual conventional, Earth-bound arguments, which totally undercut everything he'd been saying. So although he gave a really interesting talk and seemed to be well-meaning and non-dogmatic — vastly preferable to what had gone on in centuries past — I didn't buy the book.

I hope he stayed for the talk by the next speaker, philosopher AC Grayling. The church location was a bit odd for an atheist, as he acknowledged, but it was also reassuring that in this more secular age such an odd juxtaposition of speakers was accepted without a murmur. Grayling was just as charismatic and awesome as Janina Ramirez had been and his fascinating talk, *Troubled Times: Learning from the Age of Genius,* transported us from the medieval mindset to the beginning of modern thinking: the Enlightenment or Age of Reason.

Every literary work I'd ever studied or been moved by — poems, essays, novels, plays; Shakespeare's *Macbeth*, Brecht's *Galileo*, Marlow's *Faust* — all were there in this dizzying, wide-ranging talk. Nothing I'd learned from reading those often challenging texts had been a waste of time and although not always appreciated at the time, had earned me a small place in this impressive community of thinkers.

I lined up to buy his book, to which he added, just above his signature, a wry reference to Donald Trump. If ever we needed a new Age of Reason, it was now. How on earth, I wondered, did we get from that scientific explosion in the Age of Reason to the eradication of reason in today's Age of Fox News? Perhaps the last part of that question itself provides an answer, along with social media and Russian bots.

Thankfully, however, both reason and the arts were thriving in Chipping Campden, it having been a hotbed of the Arts and Crafts movement around the turn of the 20th century. Now summer had arrived, we had no need to go far to enjoy the delights of those walled rose gardens, rambling orchards, many-hued herbaceous borders and mysterious gates leading to who knows where, so beloved by the Arts and Crafts folk.

One such nearby gem was Hidcote Manor. The house itself wasn't open to the public, apart from the entryway through the sitting room with its '20s furniture and jazz-age music, but this opened onto a series of gardens managed by the National Trust. Closest to the house were the formal gardens organized as a series of outdoor rooms, each with its own distinctive personality. My favourite was the mind-blowing Red Garden, a riot of purples, burnt oranges and flaming reds.

Beyond the garden rooms were vegetable gardens, apple orchards, velvety lawns and shady trees with views over the surrounding wheat fields. We were glad we'd shipped our picnic set as this would be the perfect spot to sit out on a sunny day with a bottle of cloudy cider, some cheddar cheese and a view of, well, anything really. Everything and everywhere was achingly beautiful at Hidcote. On the other hand with the lively local pub, the Ebrington Arms, practically next door and the likelihood of a friendly drink with neighbours, why bother lugging a picnic set up hill and down dale? That was the thing about this part of the world — an excess of choices — all of them good.

But the jewel in the crown, at least for lovers of English eccentricity, was the quirky and absolutely sublime Snowshill Manor. Thanks to its late owner, the extremely weird Charles Paget Wade, we now have this rambling house full to the brim with thousands of his collectibles arranged in themed rooms, with the sole purpose of showcasing all the stuff he'd collected over decades from every corner of the world. What with heavily rigged model sailing ships, Samurai suits and penny farthing bicycles, the question that loomed over all these rooms full of clutter was: Who did — nay, who *does* — the dusting?

Second question: Where did anyone sleep? Every room in the manor was chock-a-block with harps, spinning wheels and dusty, carved wooden chests. It seemed that while his many guests 'enjoyed' sleeping in one of the manor's creepy, ancient four-poster beds, Wade — and after his marriage, his long-suffering wife — lived in the poky but equally quirky priest's house in the courtyard outside. It must have been bone-chillingly cold and depressingly dark, with no mod cons like electricity or gas. It was fascinating trying to imagine his lifestyle, with him settling into his wooden bucket chair in the cold flag-stoned kitchen on a winter's evening to read by lamplight before making his way to his little box bed, surrounded by forbidding-looking religious artefacts such as bishops' crosiers, sombre paintings and grim-faced statues.

Throughout the latter part of his life he dressed in 17th century kit and managed to find someone to cut his hair into a kind of bushy pageboy. At least he managed to *keep* his hair that seemed, according to the photos, to have maintained its shape pretty well considering he had no hair dryer, not to mention any electricity to run one even if he did. Perhaps he slept in curlers and a hair net or tied it up in rags. With his love of theatre and dressing-up, he surely had a well-stocked hair and makeup kit.

The hillside garden was a bit like Hidcote's, designed as a series of stone-walled or hedged rooms but with quirky lines of poetry appearing in odd places — a kind of fantastical *Gormenghast*. Excessive, sheer madness — and sheer delight.

A value-added benefit of walking through the fields surrounding Campden was discovering the fun of foraging. Living in the heart of the English countryside for a whole year allowed us to experience all four seasons just as farmers do, something we'd never been able to appreciate fully when living in towns and cities.

With each season came different crops and opportunities for doing a little furtive harvesting along the well-trodden edges of the fields, all in the interests of scientific enquiry of course. Broad beans, courgettes and peas in summer; blackberries in autumn (sadly pumpkins aren't found lying about on the edges of fields and are too big to carry furtively anyway); the odd broccoli stalk and kale leaf in winter; and in spring — not for foraging but definitely for eating in pubs — asparagus.

One good walk through such fields and up a gently sloping hill was to Mickleton. Since this was on the road between Campden and Stratford-upon-Avon, we knew we could always catch a bus home, especially if we'd spent a bit too long in one of Mickleton's attractive pubs, the most memorable being the Three Ways Hotel, home to the famous Pudding Club. However, we had no idea as to the eccentricity and deliciousness of this hotel until some friends stayed there while visiting the area.

As they discovered, a couple of evenings a week the restaurant held a pudding tasting, featuring all the English favourites we know and love: sticky toffee, summer pudding, jam roly-poly, spotted dick. And they didn't do things by halves. They also had a number of pudding bedrooms. We'd wondered why our friends had been so keen for us to see their room the morning we picked them up for a walk to Hidcote. That is, until we saw it.

Imagine a treacle sponge bedroom and bathroom — a bed with a golden syrup bedspread bedecked with a dripping treacle canopy; Lyle's lions featured in the wall art, curtain fittings and shower curtains. The summer pudding room might possibly have been restful but the mind boggled wondering what nightmares the spotted dick room might conjure up.

I started considering how I might design one, Aussie style. I pictured a lemon meringue pie room with billowing white curtains, soft yellow sheets and a knobbly quilted bedspread. Or perhaps a lamington room with chocolate-coloured walls, brown and white speckled curtains and jam-red stripes on the coverlet. Or how about something typically American — say, a pumpkin pie room, all squishy orange quilts and pastry-brown curtains?

Madly excessive, eccentric but so much fun — and vastly preferable to Charles Wade's claustrophobic little box bed and spooky antique four-posters.

Summer was drawing to an end but its sweet excess was not. The fruits of the orchards, hives and fields would soon to be transformed into cider, honey and jam.

Although occasionally reminded through the news and when visiting historical sites of the bitter, herd-like religious and political excesses of both past and present, those long summer Cotswold days allowed us to enjoy a few more country rambles and lingering evenings in pub gardens before the days grew shorter, darker and colder.

9. We Gather Together

Early autumn in the Cotswolds is golden — Keats' season of 'mellow fruitfulness' with honey-gold stone buildings, wheat fields ripe for harvest, heavy corncobs, pumpkins of every shape and size — and cider.

The best place for this was at the medieval half-timbered Fleece Inn, now owned by the National Trust but still a working pub. Although cramped and a little bit spooky inside — Charles Wade would have been in his element — its orchard was the perfect place to spend a leisurely afternoon, especially on a Sunday and especially when there was entertainment. Only in England could you sit at rough wooden tables eating roast beef and Yorkshire pudding with wasps circling glasses of delicious but weirdly dark-orange cider while listening to a singer called Betsy Harmony in a red and white checked country and western outfit, surrounded by bales of hay and belting out songs from the '40s.

It was an unlikely setting for those American oldies but goodies: Dean Martin, the Andrew Sisters, Doris Day, which added to the fun. But even more heart-warming was the skinny but agile little boy who had his father up dancing to every song: 'The Bugle Boy from Company B', 'In the Mood' and calling out for *More!* whenever Betsy finished each set.

Pubs like these, where families and communities come together in their shared love of sunny weather, song — and cider — are sadly a rarity in cities today. We were grateful to be part of it, at least for a while.

It was easy to fall into conversation at pubs like the Fleece, at Campden's film nights, the coffee shop, on walks — anywhere really. And apart from the general willingness to chat, what surprised us was the sheer number of people who either had lived in the US and Australia, or if not, had friends or family who did. It really brought home to us how close these historical and cultural connections still remain.

Another surprise was the level of shock expressed by the rise of Donald Trump. This was pretty well ubiquitous. I don't think we met a single person, either in the UK or in Europe, who thought otherwise. We'd had much the same reaction regarding George Bush at the time of the Iraq War but feelings now ran much higher with most people both incredulous and appalled.

It was a different story though with Brexit. As the referendum hadn't yet taken place, it was a hot topic of discussion with about a third of the people we spoke to planning on voting to leave — but reluctantly. Their love of Europe competed with their fear of being subsumed by the wave of immigrants heading west from Eastern Europe and the Middle East. Another third were totally conflicted and wished the whole referendum would vanish away. Their attitude was that understanding all the intricacies, pros and cons, was the politicians' job, not that of the man in the street. The rest were either firm leavers, mainly for the reason given above, or firm remainers, keen to remain part of the European project.

I've since wondered what the outcome might have been if the referendum had been held a year or so after Donald Trump's election and there'd been time to witness his fawning on foes and fighting with friends. With the US no longer a trustworthy ally, the need for Europeans to stick together might possibly have changed the eventual razor-thin outcome.

We had always intended for Chipping Campden to be our base for Merlinesque adventures but we couldn't tear ourselves away from our beloved Cotswolds until autumn, when we were offered a dog sit in Herefordshire's Golden Valley on the Welsh Borders.

The Golden Valley had always been a favourite, both for its beautiful walks and for its famous town of books, Hay on Wye. We'd spent memorable days in years past at Hay's annual literature festival, attending talks and browsing the many second-hand bookshops. One year was particularly memorable when, unannounced, Salman Rushdie appeared to speak at an event slated for a completely different author. As he had just published *The Satanic Verses* for which he had been placed under fatwa by Iran, he was naturally very cautious about attending public events. This subterfuge, which took everyone in the audience by surprise, was also very welcome. I'm unsure now who the advertised speaker was but there was no doubt that everyone was thrilled at having the chance to hear from the elusive and besieged Salman Rushdie.

Our autumn pet sit was in Dorstone, a tiny village a few miles from Hay, and our charge was Pip, a cute miniature Schnauzer. Pip, freshly shampooed, clipped and groomed for our stay, was very well behaved, apart from some straining on the lead when we walked down village lanes bordered with tempting hedges that harboured all kinds of small animal life. He'd join us in the sitting room at night, either on a mat before the fire or on his special chair. Owners Colin and Gloria had told us he was not allowed to go upstairs and, much to our amazement, he never did but would sit patiently in the hall waiting for us to come down. At night he cheerfully went to his bed in the kitchen and stayed there till we opened the door in the morning. Bliss is a well-trained dog!

Dorstone was a true farmers' village and the cottage was as close to a farmhouse as I'd ever been in my life. There were flourishing vegetable gardens and an orchard in one half of the garden, flowerbeds and a barbeque in the other, with a brook rushing behind a low stone wall at the bottom.

By day and if at home, we stayed in the kitchen where the Aga took pride of place. This not only kept us warm but also gave us ample opportunity to exercise our brains in figuring out how to cook on it. I hadn't been so close to the earth and the self-sufficient lifestyle since the late '70s when I was briefly into macramé, pottery, weaving and duck keeping. My pathetic attempts at these various crafts ended up in the bin and the two aggressive ducks in Sydney's duck pond. Now I had my chance to give 'the good life' a second try.

Each morning for breakfast we picked raspberries, blackberries and the last of the blueberries in the netted vegetable and fruit beds. For dinner we managed to roast some root vegetables and cook couscous on the Aga, which, we soon discovered, had only two settings: *hot* and *very hot*. It was lucky that couscous only needs boiling water and that roasted parsnips are very forgiving.

Fortunately the local pub, the Pandy, was at hand and saved us from battling too often with the Aga. For a very small, quiet village, the Pandy was surprisingly buzzing and was a great place to make friends with other villagers — and their dogs. So what with the lively scene at the Pandy, our daily walks with Pip and the Friday drop-in coffee mornings at Dorstone's Front Room, a volunteer-run set-up in what used to be the post office where locals could sit and chat over coffee, cake and bacon rolls, we soon knew almost everyone in the village.

But our love affair with the Borders nearly came to a sorry end with our attempt to follow one of the appallingly written maps in our *AA Walking Guide to Britain*.

It wasn't as if we hadn't been warned. We knew the dangers of going too far and relying too greatly on these maps. We'd spent many a wet and miserable time in the past following their limited instructions which were simply too brief and the maps too scanty to ever follow without getting lost at least once. The one I'd chosen looked just right, relatively short and skirting the beautiful Valley Dore with a couple of villages en route, which would surely minimise the chance of getting lost.

However, about a third of the way through the walk with poor little Pip in tow who, according to Gloria and Colin, was very lazy so only needed short walks, we found ourselves utterly and completely lost. We'd followed the directions to the letter up to the point where it seemed we'd have to climb a fence and cut through what looked like a very private farmyard with a couple of ferocious-sounding dogs. Since this looked — and sounded — so forbidding, we assumed the map hadn't been updated for a while or maybe it was simply wrong. It wouldn't have been the first time, as we well knew. So we decided the best thing would be to head uphill, skirt around the farm, and then see if the directions became clearer.

They didn't. The further we went, the *less* clear the directions became. In the end we gave up, realising we'd obviously gone astray way back at 'Forbidden Farm' and we now had two choices: backtrack, even though we'd face the same problem all over again, or press on and hope for the best.

We decided on the second choice but sadly there *was* no best and not a single welcoming village or pub as far as the eye could see. We couldn't check the GPS on our phones as we were out of range and our compass was back in the car. Now off the hillside we found ourselves wandering aimlessly down a network of lanes lined with such tall hedges that we didn't have a clue what was around us. At last, trying a different tack and heading off-piste, we found ourselves in an even worse predicament, staggering up one steep field and down another, only to find barbed wire fences at the bottom, completely overgrown with nettles and blackberry canes — and no way out.

Forced to backtrack, negotiating rotting wooden fences and putrid mud puddles, with storm clouds brewing and Pip covered from head to toe in green slime and cow dung, we came upon what looked like the set of that horror movie set in the Australian outback, *Wolf Creek*, in which a group of American backpackers meet their doom.

At the top of the hill, a few tumbledown stone farm buildings and sheds appeared, surrounded by what looked like part open-air industrial museum and part city dump. Rusting relics of agricultural tools and machinery lay about, seemingly abandoned and covered in weeds. I had visions of being attacked from behind, stunned and shoved into one of those crumbling ruins, never to be seen again.

Suddenly, coming from somewhere amongst the abandoned farm machinery, collapsing sheds and rotting mattresses, we heard a whirring sound.

Memories of that scary medieval tale, *Gawain and the Green Knight*, came instantly to mind — the bit where Sir Gawain, expecting to get his head chopped off, turns up at the isolated Green Chapel to the ominous sound of the Green Knight sharpening his axe.

That was set in the West Country too. And had creepy stone buildings. And tools like axe-sharpening stones. And a longhaired scary-looking person emerging from the mill, ready to do his worst! Pip though, in his new slime-green incarnation, which no doubt would be very attractive to a Green Knight, might possibly escape such a grisly fate and find a new home.

Richard, not having read *Gawain and the Green Knight*, was fortunately ignorant of these potential horrors so went to investigate and sure enough, such a person appeared. But instead of long green hair, beard and very sharp axe he had long white hair, beard and a rather ferocious dog — and thankfully had only been fixing the barn roof, not sharpening his axe blade.

He pointed us to the far corner of what one might generously call a field where we discovered a broken-down stile shrouded by huge blackberry canes with thorns as long as my fingers. This was going to be tricky and was made even trickier with us having to carry Pip through this thorny Iron Maiden. Almost impaling ourselves on the jagged, broken wood of the stile below and the rampant blackberry thorns in the hedges above, we finally made it to civilisation.

Pip patiently suffered through two baths and a thorough scrubbing that evening but even then we feared his formerly beautifully groomed coat would be permanently tinged with green.

Fearing to trust the AA guides again, we abandoned further proposed walks in Wales and instead opted to visit some safer, impeccably mapped National Trust properties.

Croft Castle, set high on a hill near the market town of Leominster, was particularly fascinating because of its genealogy and its geology. In the upstairs hall was a huge family tree covering a whole wall and it was interesting to see how many branches ended up in Australia and New Zealand. Again, it really brought home how close the historical connections are with these countries. Two of the most recent additions were 'Brett' and 'Sharon'. No prizes for guessing which was their country and decade of birth.

Another common feature that kept cropping up in so many of these National Trust estates was the number of sons lost in the First World War and particularly Gallipoli. It certainly made me realise that the ANZACS weren't alone in losing their young men in that disastrous debacle. The toffs of England and Wales did too.

But the best part of our Croft Castle visit, apart from seeing a replica stuffed boar's head taking pride of place on the dining room's banquet table, was communing with nature on the Fishponds walk. With few visitors venturing through the cowpats and mud to the river, we time-travelled to days when life was lived closer to nature and at a much slower pace. I imagined the Croft kids in the 1920s spending idyllic summers leaping from the stout branches of those ancient trees to swim in the ferny stream-fed ponds, with the afternoon sun slanting through the last of the autumn leaves.

Old lime pits, kilns and dams, all now picturesque ruins, were reminders of the estate's days as a bustling industrial site, while signage told of its geological history going back millions of years to when this part of England was subtropical. Although Pip would have been in heaven checking out the mud and cowpats, we left him at home to enjoy his garden. Later we would reward him with good company around the barbeque, followed by a Welsh 'dragon sausage' from the butcher's shop at Hay on Wye but we had also saved him from another scouring in the laundry tub.

A couple of weeks later back in Chipping Campden, we decided to make the most of the last tawny autumn days and explore other parts of Gloucestershire. A new town for us, described by the Guardian newspaper as a 'spirited community', was Stroud. Recommended by the artistically inclined Brill couple, we found it to be just as they had claimed: pleasantly edgy, not too big and not too small, and with a good jazz scene.

One Saturday, being market day, Halloween and unusually sunny for that time of year, we decided that it was the perfect time to check it out. Even though I knew Stroud was on the River Frome I was still surprised to see just how steep and hilly it was. I could see too why it would have appealed to the artsy, unconventional Brill couple. As one of a handful of the UK's 'transition towns', it aimed to reduce carbon emissions by creating networks for the sale of locally sourced produce and the communal sharing of skills. From the happy faces and vibrant vibe, I'd say it was definitely working. It had a real buzz and a sense of common purpose.

Our first stop anywhere is always for coffee and although the shop with 'a yawn is a silent scream for coffee' sign out front appealed, the Black Book Café, despite being higher up the hill, really seemed to fit the bill. It was bigger than most coffee shops with every wall lined with bookshelves that extended right up to its high ceilings. The books were divided into categories making it easy to find something to your taste — historical fiction, fantasy or whatever.

We were very lucky to squeeze in though, what with the crowd in town for the special Halloween market as well as it seeming to be such a popular spot for locals to gather. Eavesdropping on a nearby table, we heard a couple planning what sounded like being an impressively big arts festival that was to be held soon, with under-pavement heating and loads of theatrical spaces. Sitting behind us on a battered sofa were a couple of teachers having a good old natter while delving into a huge communal yarn basket on the floor beside them to do a spot of knitting. It was a bit hard working out exactly what the communal knitting project was meant to be but it was long and extremely colourful. I would have quite enjoyed knitting a few rows myself.

Once no longer desperate for coffee, we wandered downhill to the market to mingle with the rest of the townsfolk and check out the local produce, home-baked

goods and weird Halloween hats. Arts, crafts and books —
yes, it did indeed seem to be a spirited community. So
after buying a couple of seasonal venison pies and
Christmas puddings, and with dark clouds gathering, it
was time to head home to our somewhat more sedate, but
equally charming, Chipping Campden.

10. Lashings of Wind, Rain and Pudding

Winter in England. What's left to say? Short cold days, heavy grey skies, rain and mud. Many National Trust properties close for winter, not just because there's little to see in the gardens but also to carry out repairs and refurbishments, so we'd agreed to do a pet sit in Cornwall for a change of scenery, swapping Gloucestershire's barren fields for Cornwall's wild waves.

This pet sitting assignment was in Wadebridge near the Camel River on Cornwall's chilly northern coast. The owners ran their home as a B&B so we knew the accommodation would be of a pretty good standard, which would be very important when stuck indoors on those long winter evenings. They were heading off to an Airbnb conference in Paris, a great choice since it's enjoyable no matter what the weather, and it was being held at a most convenient time, Cornwall's low season, so they could have a little holiday as well.

The house was in a good location, being just a gentle walk downhill to the town of Wadebridge and the Camel estuary. It was sturdy, built to withstand harsh Cornish winters, and surrounded by what were pretty gardens judging from the summertime photos, but a bit barren and bedraggled at that time of year.

It was a relief though to find that inside, the house itself certainly didn't disappoint. Downstairs was a conservatory where the owners would serve breakfast to their B&B guests and a large, well-organized kitchen with breakfast bar and sitting area that was warm and cosy in the early evenings while cooking and chatting. Happily there was no Aga so cooking wouldn't be quite as hit and miss as it had been in Dorstone. In the evenings we could sit in the sitting room beyond the hall with its big squashy sofas, fireplace and TV. Upstairs were two good-sized guest bedrooms decorated in dark blue and white, and a sparkling seaside-inspired bathroom.

Jet, the young black Labrador, was something of a handful but very endearing. He was ball mad and his energy for chasing them in the nearby park or down on the Camel River walk was inexhaustible. His bed and toy box were in the kitchen sitting area and every day around dusk, just as I was trying to prepare dinner, he would get his second wind and insist on playing a tug-of-war game with his collection of ropes, scraps of cloth and pig skins.

One thing that particularly impressed us was Jet's obedience to the not-going-upstairs rule. Before leaving for Paris, the owners had told us that he wasn't allowed further than the bottom of the hall stairs, a rule we didn't really expect him to obey after we'd spent a day dealing with his ball-chasing and rope-tugging antics. But on that first night as we turned out the lights and headed upstairs to our room, he stood at the foot of the stairs, looked wistfully up at us and then padded back to his kitchen bed. And there he stayed, thankfully, until morning.

Tiggy the cat lived a more independent life, moving from one sunny chair to another with an occasional spot of outside roaming and was almost an afterthought, apart from one awful occasion. My friend Liz had driven from Devon to visit and had brought along her two dogs whose keen interest in Tiggy was definitely not reciprocated. Much to my dismay, after a couple of hours of these unwanted attentions, Tiggy took off through the cat flap and vanished into the darkness. All that night I barely got a wink of sleep, worried that she'd been so miffed at being displaced by Liz's dogs that she'd run away, never to return, and somehow I'd have to break this terrible news to her owners. Next morning, bleary-eyed and tousle-haired, I went down to the kitchen and there she was — curled up in her favourite kitchen chair as if nothing had happened. I could have kissed her but instead, with great relief, got her breakfast.

But that little drama was nothing compared to what was to come.

Storm Abigail, an unwelcome guest, dominated our week's stay. But another very welcome guest was our Brisbane-based son Andrew who, unexpectedly having to fly to London on business, came to join us for a few days.

He arrived late in the afternoon, jet-lagged and exhausted from the flight, followed by the long drive from Heathrow to Cornwall, so headed to bed early. But, as anyone who has travelled long haul across multiple time zones understands, he was wide awake at 2 a.m. so spent those empty pre-dawn hours checking his emails — and the news.

I'd woken up early myself from the racket of all the rain, so not wanting to disturb anyone, turned on my laptop for a quiet early-morning read. I couldn't believe what I was seeing. The Paris attacks on the Stade de France and the carnage at the Bataclan were splashed across the headlines.

Just then, while this horror was sinking in, Andrew appeared at my bedroom door and tentatively asked, 'Where did you say the owners were going?'

We emailed them straight away to see if they were alright which, fortunately, they were. Unfortunately though, their hotel was practically next door to the Bataclan and was in lock-down. So conference cancelled and no holiday but mercifully, at least they were safe and sound.

Wadebridge, like Stroud, was another hilly town but on a much gentler slope and with the river much wider as it flowed through the estuary to the sea. It was hard to imagine the horrors that had taken place in Paris or the monsters who had perpetrated them, while living in this peaceful, neighbourly town where everyone we met seemed happy to chat and pass the time of day. We'd take Jet to one of the coffee shops before his walk along the river and again, his behaviour was impeccable. He'd sit patiently tied to a chair while we sat huddled against the cold, trying to warm our hands around the coffee cups. Once on his walk though, it was a different story. This is when we appreciated Andrew's visit even more. He'd found the walk beside the Camel River so appealing that he offered to take Jet there for a run most mornings, even in the rain, and give him a good work out.

Since Andrew had come all the way from London and wanted to see not just us but Cornwall, we rugged up and headed out each day, usually with Jet in tow, to see the sights. We endured Abigail's blasting wind at Watergate Bay where Jet was in his Labrador element, chasing balls along the beach, running into the surf with other dogs and searching for lost balls in rock pools. It was a surprise watching how determined he was to retrieve them, bravely sticking his head, nearly up to the neck, into the freezing water.

Padstow, Looe — every town we visited was lashed by Storm Abigail's fury but we did find one or two nice eating spots and keeping true to the British spirit, we didn't grumble. We were grateful to have had an unexpected reunion and a nice warm house to come back to each day — and that we weren't in Paris.

∾

One day we drove to a little place called Duloe, between Liskeard and Looe, to check out a potential Christmas pet sit. It sounded like a dream assignment on the website — a converted mill, tumbling stream, leafy woods. The photos looked lovely too — a picturesque stone building, pleasant sitting room with open fireplace and a modern kitchen.

Thank heavens we saw it before committing.

The sturdy wooden front door seemed welcoming enough, as did the two ladies who greeted us, but once inside I was beset with a sense of unease. Squashed in the hallway under the stairs to the right was a rabbit hutch. To the left was a bedroom-cum-animal sanctuary complete with dog crate, dog bed, a huge cat climbing frame that dominated the window, an aquarium full of newts and toads, and atop the wardrobe, piled high to the ceiling, scores of stuffed toys. To literally top it off, the bed too was heaped with stuffed toys and cushions, obviously another cat hangout. The other, smaller bedroom wasn't much of an improvement.

The mill was laid out over three levels with a child barrier on every landing so that when climbing the stairs, it felt like being trapped in a prison tower. Once upstairs in the sitting room we were shown the aquarium full of tropical fish and we met the dog. Now the dog was nice enough and would have been fine on his own. But the cats, newts, toads, fish and rabbits — every fibre of my being was screaming NO!

The two ladies were so pleasant and were so much looking forward to a two-week skiing trip, that I was really torn. But dealing with that menagerie in the depths of an English winter, deep in a valley with no easy escape to a jolly pub down the road, seemed a recipe for very miserable Christmas indeed.

After spending the whole trip back to Wadebridge agonizing over what to do, we decided to politely withdraw our application and they just as politely accepted the inevitable. They'd told us when we were there how hard it was to find sitters and we certainly could understand why. We'd learnt a huge lesson about the importance of checking a potential sit, in person when possible, before accepting. Even so, it's unrealistic to expect perfection a hundred percent of the time but when comparing this dreary animal-filled mill to our comfortable cottage in Chipping Campden, it really would have been a bridge too far.

We celebrated our lucky escape the next day with a delicious fish lunch at the Old Sail Loft in Looe, a welcome respite from the storm outside, before bidding farewell to both Cornwall and Andrew, and heading home to the Cotswold Hills.

Chipping Campden had been tastefully decorated for Christmas, just as you'd expect from this very traditional Cotswold village. Silvery lights decked the old Market Hall, candied orange and cinnamon wreaths welcomed visitors on cottage doors, and Santa's sleigh took pride of place atop the Town Hall roof.

Hidcote, mostly deserted at this time of year, was still worth a visit, with its rich earth ready for new plantings, spicy Christmas cake in the tearoom, spidery black branches dramatic against grey skies and the odd robin redbreast pecking amongst dead leaves and tree trunks.

It was also the season for visiting Christmas markets. The most sparkling and buzzing of all was in Bath with its moodily lit abbey dominating the market square and its bare-branched trees, now bedecked with fairy lights, creating a magical Christmas forest.

Heading there with friends one stormy evening, we jumped puddles, hung on to battered brollies, succumbed to the delights of huge lengths of liquorice and chunks of chocolate honeycomb, and were tempted by hut after Christmas hut offering mulled wine and cider. Even in all that rain and cold, the market was worth the effort, though it wasn't easy finding a table in any of the crowded pubs when clutching umbrellas with frozen fingers became too much to bear.

But apart from visiting Christmas markets, how, we wondered, might we spend Christmas itself, now that we'd bailed from the Cornish mill menagerie?

The perfect solution appeared as if by magic — cat sitting in the Netherlands. We'd still have mills and though not water-powered, there was something to be said for windmills standing proudly in Holland's flat landscape versus water mills deep in Cornwall's soggy, shadowy valleys, especially in winter.

Although we would have been happy hunkering down for Christmas in the Cotswolds, a last-minute listing by Jacky, a Scottish lass living in Leiden, had caught my eye. She was working in this university town, living in a renovated merchant's house with one — let me repeat — *one* — cat called Monkey. She wanted to visit her family in Scotland so needed a cat sitter from Christmas Eve till just after New Year's Day.

It was going to be tight, arriving on Christmas Eve and with no Christmas dinner organized but we had our stash of Christmas puddings from the Stroud Christmas market and were optimistic that with a quick dash around Leiden's local shops we'd have enough supplies to see us through Christmas Day. Our main worry was wondering if and where we'd find custard — absolutely essential for an English Christmas pudding — and something sparkling to drink. Forget the turkey.

By the time we arrived in Leiden and Jacky had shown us the ropes, it was nearly dark with little time to shop before everything closed for Christmas. Luckily the shops weren't too far away so we made a mad dash to a supermarket, which we figured would be the easiest to negotiate with no Dutch in our linguistic repertoire — this being before we realized that the Dutch were completely bilingual — and grabbed what we could for our Christmas feast.

It really was slim pickings at that time of day, and on that day in particular, but we managed to nab a couple of bottles of Kir Royale, some smoked salmon, ham on the bone, avocado, asparagus and strawberries. This would require even less effort than our Goring Christmas dinner since it would be entirely cold — apart from our Stroud Christmas puddings which, much to our relief, would now be accompanied by a carton of *vla* — Dutch custard.

Leiden was certainly a great spot to spend Christmas. It was a pretty university town with quite a history, so interesting in itself, but was also close to most places we wanted to visit. And like all Dutch towns, it was full of bikes. Bikes were everywhere, including the ones occasionally blown into the canals, which wasn't so surprising with all that wind. What was even more interesting was the number of cars parked so close to the edges of the canals. How did the drivers get out without falling in? Not to mention the cars themselves. I'm glad it wasn't me having to attempt it. Reverse parking in a normal street was tricky enough without the fear of a watery grave. Jacky lived just a few steps from such a canal so we were able to witness many such parking feats on our daily walks.

This traditional white merchant's house had three floors with an open-plan living room and modern kitchen downstairs and wooden staircase curving upstairs to our bedroom which had French windows and a cat flap opening onto a roof garden. After our earlier dog experiences we were a bit disconcerted to find a cat bed in the corner of the room but we rarely saw Monkey actually in it. It was a bit of a mystery exactly where, or if, she slept at night. But from the sound of the cat flap banging shortly after we went to bed and then seeing her sitting downstairs in the morning, we figured she was spending quite a few hours roaming around the neighbouring rooftops.

The only time we actually saw her in the bedroom at night was on New Year's Eve. Well, not so much saw her as felt her. We'd gone to bed, optimistically hoping to get some sleep despite the wall-to-wall fireworks the Dutch seemed so keen on. They'd started up around midday and went on through the evening, reaching a crescendo at midnight but still continued on … and on. At one particularly rackety point, I felt something heavy at the bottom on the bed. Of course it was Monkey, too frightened by the barrage of whistling fireworks to head out for her usual nocturnal prowl. But despite my aversion to animals on beds, I didn't have the heart to turf her off.

After all that dog walking and ball throwing, we found cat sitting a bit of a doddle. Since Monkey wasn't confined to quarters, we could spend days out exploring without worrying about her. We fed her morning and evening, cleaned her litter tray and enjoyed seeing her sitting in the net-curtained window each afternoon on our return. Although she kept to herself in the main, sometimes she'd invite us to play a chasing game. She'd begin by standing on the stairs peering through the railings and then, the minute we approached, would dart upstairs to the landing, pause while waiting for us to follow, and then scamper up to the attic. No wonder her name was Monkey.

We thought Leiden was a pretty cool town until we saw Delft. There was a wonderful little museum with a range of exhibits dedicated to Vermeer and as an unexpected bonus, its café was our first introduction to one of Holland's other great attractions — Dutch apple cake. From then on, every day began with a search for a café that served a hot, strong flat white and a really tart, fruity apple cake.

Not only did Delft charm us with its great art, coffee and apple cake but also with the funky shops and unexpected community art that seemed to pop up in every town square. There were clothing shops where you could buy a glass of wine, furniture shops with cafés, and hairdressers that looked like pages out of a kids' colouring book. It was well worth the train trip from Leiden — the whole fifteen minutes of it.

The only problem with Delft — and indeed every other Dutch town with their trendy shops, cafés and bars — was that we started to feel somewhat ancient. No one seemed to be older than twenty-five. Ragged, knee-less jeans were still fashionable it seemed while ours didn't look trendily ragged but more sad, old-geezer frayed. We didn't have blue hair or nose piercings or smoke weed, which, as we quickly discovered, was an integral part of the Dutch café culture. In short, we felt a bit out of it. Maybe all the people our age lived in the suburbs. Or they were all dead from decades of weed smoking. But despite being so ancient and fashion-free, we were treated very politely by the Dutch youngsters and were rarely stared at, apart from the time we nearly entered a seedy-looking 'café' only to beat a hasty retreat.

৵

Eventually however, we did come across someone of our age group in the Aussie-inspired Drover's Dog Tavern in Amsterdam where we were staying for a couple of days before heading back to the UK. By this time we'd become used to unusual combinations of bars in furniture showrooms and cafés in men's outfitters. This place though, was something else again, with its strange, vaguely Australian menu featuring items like roast kangaroo and chickpea-and-beetroot burgers.

But the highlight was the rock 'n roll band. The guitarist and drummer seemed normal enough, that is, they were in their twenties with slashed jeans and blue hair. But the lead singer was something else again.

Imagine a hunched, dissipated, pasty-faced, stringy-haired version of an ageing '60s rock star with a kind of Chris Rea/Rod Stewart voice but ruined by decades of hard smoking, sex and drugs — and tuneless to boot. He started by saying he'd worked in Perth, Sydney and Brisbane for years before moving to Amsterdam but his pronunciation of 'BrisBANE' let the jumbuck out of the tucker-bag. Imposter! I suppose though, being an Australian-themed tavern, he felt the need to strengthen his Aussie credentials, despite actually being an American.

We were totally gob-smacked — and totally won over by him and his band, the Grandpa Death Experience. And as a bonus, we now felt a little superior comparing our equally aged but much healthier appearance to his, though Richard did envy his black pork-pie hat and mustard-yellow shoes.

Our last night in the Netherlands was spent at the Fashion Hotel indulging in a cocktail up in the Sky Bar where I again felt my age. Far from enjoying a relaxing drink gazing out over the view, we were blasted with — well, what I'd describe as monotonous thumping racket.

From that moment on, I knew I was past my sell-by date. When it comes to cocktail bars, I prefer the smooth strains of mellow jazz rather than the pounding of a heavy bass. And a nice slice of warm apple cake or Christmas pudding (with custard) is vastly preferable to weed.

FRENCH FOLLIES, FANTASIES AND FRIENDSHIPS

11. Chains and Châtelains

Along with spring came our departure from the Chipping Campden cottage. After all that agonizing the previous year trying to find just the right place for our home base, it had exceeded all our expectations. The village was beautiful, even in the middle of winter, and was within a day's drive of other attractive spots: Cornwall, Wales and of course Oxford. It had been easy to lock up and leave, allowing us to do a few extended house sits.

As incurable Francophiles, we'd been tempted by a couple of intriguing offers in parts of France where we'd not been before. The first of these was on the outskirts of Fontenay-le-Comte, an hour's drive inland from La Rochelle on the Atlantic coast.

I'd seen the listing before we left Sydney and had applied on the spot, hoping against hope that we'd be the lucky couple chosen to be part of this once-in-a-lifetime venture. The château, romantically named Cristallin, looked amazing from the photos — a pale stone château with soft grey slate roof, bedrooms richly decorated with damask coverlets and bed hangings, and a sprawling garden. The owners were New Zealanders who, like us, had fallen in love with France but had gone one giant step further by investing in this charming fixer-upper *petit château* — their very own Sleeping Beauty.

The story was that they'd hoped to run it as a holiday let and had actually done so for a couple of years but had now moved on to fresh pastures: a restaurant on the Mediterranean coast. Unable to keep up with château maintenance from that distance, they needed an ongoing stream of house sitters with DIY skills to keep it in a decent state for paying guests.

After a flurry of emails it was agreed that Richard's DIY skills were exactly what they needed for the next phase of their maintenance schedule, while we were over the moon for having been chosen to share in the collective project of bringing this faded beauty back to its former glory.

We'd be taking over from a Canadian couple who were painting the window shutters, while they in turn had taken over from an Irish guy who'd spent his winter repairing the broken slats and hinges. Our duties would be wallpapering the bedrooms and doing a bit of minor electrical work in preparation for the arrival of a group that had rented the place for summer. The owners had arranged for the wallpaper to be delivered to us in Brill so we could bring it with us. However, unfortunately for the owners — though as it turned out, fortunately for us — the wallpaper hadn't arrived on time. So we headed across the Channel, minus the wallpaper but ready to take on any other suitable jobs that we could complete in our allotted three weeks.

As we drove up to Cristallin's towering metal gates, which Richard had to wrench from the ivy-encrusted walls before we could enter the drive, we began to get an inkling of why people shy away from buying such lovely old buildings. The upkeep is relentless. It's all very well being carried away by the romance of a château in the French countryside but maintaining it is a different matter — a very expensive and very time-consuming one.

There was plenty of work to be done inside what with the peeling shutters and windows, most of which were still in their original state despite the efforts of our predecessors, the old wallpaper and some minor problems with electrical fittings. It didn't seem too bad until we looked at the height of the ceilings, the intricacies of the wall fixtures, the wires running up and down every wall, and the problems with damp and mould. But once done, we thought, it would be magnificent.

That is, until we'd lived there long enough to see problem after problem appearing with the impossible layout — eight bedrooms and only two functional bathrooms — its small, out-dated kitchen and the unfortunate location.

On one side was a picturesque stone village but the church, which was practically next door, rang its bells on the hour, loudly and relentlessly — seven days a week, starting at 7 a.m. and ending at 10 p.m. — leaving a mere nine hours of peace and quiet before it started all over again. The first bell would ring seven times; there'd be a pause and then it would ring seven times again. And just in case you might have managed to drop off to sleep, it would ring three more times to make *really* sure you hadn't dropped off. Then, with a final sadistic flourish, it would ring with clanging intensity for about three minutes more.

On the other side was a newish housing estate of low-maintenance but comparatively boring little boxes. And close by that was a characterless strip of shops and a few lonely looking tower blocks standing in what had been, until recently, fields.

Then there was the garden that looked as if it was starting to become part of the château. Roots were undermining the stonework, blackberry was spreading all through what once must have been a magnificent garden and was taking over the lovely soft stone walls, and ivy was invading every nook and cranny. I love wisteria but over the years I've come to understand the need to keep it under strict control as it can undermine a whole building if left to its own devices, which here it seemed, it had.

A Sleeping Beauty indeed. But what a building! It was actually a bit spooky in a gentle sort of way. Its corner tower had been transformed into a quaint tiny round library on the ground floor, then became a romantic stone-tiled wet room on the first floor — though sadly unusable due to leaks — and ended as a mysterious locked room on the top floor.

The ground floor rooms were the easiest to live in. On one side of the wide entrance hall was a dining room and kitchen and on the other, two pleasant open-plan reception rooms and the corner tower library. Although chilly and dark in early spring, especially with all the ivy and creepers covering the windows and tall trees blocking the light, these rooms would have been lovely on hot summer days. But even though the main rooms were a good size, the kitchen was way too small to cater for big groups, while the cooker was in a shocking state, thick with black grease and goo.

The upstairs bedrooms, four on each floor, opened onto each other and were furnished with vast armoires, cabinets, antique bedsteads and one fascinating but dust-collecting pianola. I had the distinct impression that the owners, in the first flurry of excitement and optimism, had gone a bit overboard when making the rounds of the local antique shops and *brocantes* or flea markets. The château was stuffed with countless atmospheric but basically unusable pieces, while the kitchen and bathrooms barely functioned. There weren't even towel rails. No wonder the radiators were so rusty.

The first-floor bedrooms were reasonable enough, each with different patterned wall coverings, one even of silk, but all were peeling or stained so we could see why the owners wanted them repapered. It was also clear what a massive job it would be, what with the removal of the old paper, the height of the walls and the difficulty in hanging new paper around so many intricate wall fittings, wires and bed canopy fixtures. Some sections were bulging and a bit soggy, while the walls of the top-floor stairway were covered in sagging dark brown hessian with heaven knows what lumpy stuff behind it. We'd certainly been saved from a truly horrible job by the non-arrival of the new wallpaper.

We slept in the room with the biggest bed and that adjoined the tower's wet room. Even though the shower wasn't usable, at least the loo was. It didn't bother me at first but after the first few nights, this room's wallpaper began to take on a life of its own. I'd lie in the antique four-poster bed, hemmed in by both the heavy brocade bed hangings and the mustard-yellow, puce flower-sprigged wallpaper, with uneasy thoughts of the ending of that horror story, 'The Yellow Wallpaper'.

The upstairs bedrooms were spookier still. Being directly under the roof, they were more like attic rooms and the furniture was not nearly so grand. With even less light than downstairs and with such spare furnishings, not to mention the locked tower room and vast white-tiled, old-fashioned bathroom that looked like something out of

The Shining, this was a part of the house that I studiously avoided, especially if alone. I couldn't help wondering what the summer guests would think, especially those stuck with a bedroom up there. Maybe, I hoped, in summer and with a crowd, it might not be quite so forbidding.

ᕤ

After spending the first day checking the place out, we decided our priorities should be blitzing the kitchen, especially the grease-encrusted cooker, and making the garden safe. With a large group expected in a few weeks and with the gloomy interior, a pleasant outdoor living space would be really important. The pool in the back sunny corner with its few outdoor tables and chairs would be the main attraction but it was thick with dead leaves and black with mould.

The Canadian couple who'd been here before us in early spring when it was very cold and damp, had spent hours sanding and painting the lovely old wooden shutters downstairs. We'd planned on continuing their efforts now that wallpapering was impossible but as the weather was so nice and we could see the state of the garden, we thought we'd spend our first week working there instead.

This is the sort of project that can become endless, as any gardener will know. Wisteria had invaded the upstairs bathroom windows, ivy and nettles infested the gardens, blackberry runners snaked through the grass and their canes whipped out from trees and bushes. The lawn between the house and the pool was knee high and the orchard was beyond hope. The best we could do was to make it safe, especially for exploring children. Beyond the mouldy pool was a ruined orangery, now a prickly pit full of blackberry and broken glass. And what was once a charming pigeonnière was now so dilapidated that a roof tile, forced loose by invading ivy, nearly smashed on my head as I walked by.

Each morning we'd head out into the garden and work for hours, trying to bring some order to this riot of rampant nature. It became so addictive that I'd even dream of pulling out great long runners of wisteria and ivy. The hours flew by, as we'd tell ourselves — just that next wall of ivy, just a few more clumps of nettle. I'd eventually drag myself away to get some lunch, hands and wrists cut and tender from tearing out all those brambles and nettles that seemed to defy any gardening glove known to man. Richard mowed a path from the kitchen to the outdoor table, now placed in a sunny spot beside the pool (still under its winter cover) where we'd sit for a quick lunch before returning to taming our wilderness.

At 9 p.m. Richard would still be outside, hacking away at the walls of blackberry, until eventually, as the sky darkened to pitch black and stars appeared, he'd be tempted indoors. But what a sight to end the day! With luck, in a few short weeks it would be warm enough for the summer guests to sit out after dinner and enjoy that spectacular starry sky.

There was no point trying to get to sleep before the final burst from the church at 10 p.m. But then, at 7 a.m. on the dot, those wretched bells would frighten us out of our wits and our sleep and it would be time once more to don gloves and wellies to do battle with the thorns and vines of Cristallin.

⁂

The wall between Cristallin and the housing estate next door was especially thick with ivy. Richard started hacking at it one day, only to discover that an entire clothesline was buried within its depths. We'd been attempting to dry our laundry on the sagging line held up by posts between a couple of trees near the house, not realizing anything more substantial existed — not that it would have been much good trapped inside that thicket of ivy. Richard was able to get rid of some of it but as it had grown right over the top of the wall, he'd need to go next door to finish the job. So toward the end of our stay he went around to check it out. And that's when he first met our neighbours, Monsieur and Madame Leblanc, who were outside tending their neat and very orderly raised vegetable beds.

Richard's French being minimal, he came to fetch me, not only to act as interpreter but also to meet this charming couple. It was hard to believe that on one side of the wall was a neat French suburban garden while on the other was something out of a fairy tale, with its wild grounds and ivy-shrouded château. It turned out that M Leblanc had been itching to get rid of all that ivy for ages and was not only happy to allow Richard into his garden to do it, but also to lend him his chainsaw. And last but not least — help with the sawing himself.

It turned out there were four sets of neighbours backing onto the wall who gleefully took the opportunity to come over for a sticky beak at their mysterious ivy-shrouded neighbour, normally locked behind its metal gates and high walls, and have a good old chat about it. I must admit to not having a blind clue what they were talking about half the time but from all the gesticulation and occasional recognizable phrases, it seemed to revolve around huge blackberry canes, spikes, ivy stalks as thick as your arm, the possibility of the wall falling down and what would happen in a storm with all those broken slates on the pigeonnière's roof. Then as suddenly as they'd appeared they all took off, apart from M Leblanc, and left us to it.

By this stage Richard, pumped with adrenalin and confidence from all that hacking with the electric saw, bravely tried to expand on his minimal French from beyond a couple of words to whole sentences and managed to ask M Leblanc if he'd like a beer. But the really big test was to come when our neighbour invited us back to his house to share *un verre* later that afternoon. How would we get through a social situation that might last an hour or more? And how would poor Monsieur and Madame endure it? Their English was as minimal as our French.

It started well though, with an inspection of their little raised beds. I found I could actually discuss their various vegetables and herbs, even sharing tales of nettles and how they made good soup. A few *verres* of Champagne and Scotch later, we all discovered our linguistic skills had improved immensely, moving on from nettle recipes to discussing their sons and girlfriends, our son and grandsons, work, retirement and living in Australia or America compared to France. So we all survived and actually had a jolly good time. My only regret was that the next day we came down with terrible hacking coughs and sore throats. And just as that lot was clearing up, we were afflicted by even worse gastric attacks, so we were never able to reciprocate or even bid farewell to this lovely, funny and hospitable couple.

~

Decades ago in my high school French class, we read a book called *Contes et Légendes*. At the time none of us dared question such a choice of reader, though it was probably really a matter of what was available in the book room than anything else. In later years when travelling in France and struggling to order a meal or enquire about where to fix a flat tyre, it did seem a strange choice. Fairy stories and legends might be fun to read but not exactly the stuff of everyday communication.

But after spending time in Cristallin, I started to see the wisdom of that choice. Everywhere we looked we were reminded of folk tales and fairy stories. We'd also started to see more clearly — the very name 'Cristallin' refers to clear vision — the gap between fantasy and reality, and the mythical versus real-life France.

Fantasy versus reality? Let's take the dream of the French idyll — breakfasting on crisp buttery croissants and sipping a morning coffee before spending afternoons strolling in picturesque villages and browsing for bric-à-brac in quaint flea markets. And then take the reality of trying to find a café that's actually open, particularly on a Sunday or a Monday morning, and the dearth of interesting shops in places where new *supermarchés* have taken over. So often we'd drive to an attractive town ready to see the sights and either the shops were open but the museums were closed, or the museum was open but its café was closed, or it was lunch time when *everything* was closed — and variations on that theme.

Cristallin itself too, quite literally, showed us the dangers of viewing life through rose-tinted glasses. Its owners, like so many others, had bought into the reality TV *Place in the Sun* fantasy, only to have their dreams turn sour and find themselves stuck in a stagnant market with a property they couldn't sell and was too expensive to repair.

Beauty and the Beast? Look no further than the beauty of Cristallin, viewed from a distance with its pale stone walls laced in mauve wisteria, the carefully selected photos showing it sitting in the middle of a manicured lawn surrounded by leafy gardens. Then look closer and see the beastly blackberry canes with their sharp spikes; the stinging nettles; the dark English ivy swamping all it encountered, ripping into stonework and infiltrating drains; the wisteria vines attacking the windows, tearing down pipes and electrical wires.

Sleeping Beauty? The same story, with this beautiful castle, gradually succumbing to nature and hidden from view, just waiting to be brought back to life. We couldn't help but wonder what this place once was and what it could become once again.

Cinderella? That was me, scrubbing the winter's algae and mould from the sides of the pool, raking up piles of nettles and scouring the grease-encrusted cooker.

Brer Rabbit in the Briar Patch? That was Richard battling the huge blackberry canes, chopping them into pieces and chucking them into the broken concrete pit that had once been an elegant orangery.

Hunchback of Notre Dame? That was me, suffering from the *grippe gastrique* and trying to get a bit of kip after the 10 p.m. bell ringing, knowing that in a few short hours the clanging would start all over again. I had visions of throttling the bell-ringer but in a kind of role reversal. I'd be the crazed hunchback, though hunched from griping pains rather than a deformed spine.

It wasn't all weeding and hacking though. We'd decided that if we worked for two days then it would be fair to have one day to ourselves, which we mostly spent on the nearby Atlantic coast. It seemed as if this coast had two sides — light and dark. There was the beauty of the ocean, the honey-coloured medieval buildings of the Vendée, the fresh oysters and the crisp Muscadet. There was also the fascinating history of towns such as Nantes, La Rochelle and Bordeaux.

But that's where the dark side came in. These towns, apart from being popular places to visit, were also France's chief ports in the slave trade — the notorious triangular trade. Ships would carry manufactured goods such as cloth and guns to be sold in Africa where cargoes of slaves would be taken on board, destined for the West Indies' slave markets. The ships then completed their triangular voyage, carrying cargoes of sugar, coffee and tobacco back to these Atlantic ports.

Nantes hadn't hidden away its horrible history but rather had done the reverse, erecting a sobering memorial to the abolition of slavery on the very quays from where the slave ships had sailed off to trade in their cargoes of human misery. The impressive Museum of the History of Nantes too, had rooms devoted to this theme, giving an in-depth account of the slave trade and the conditions under which the enslaved people had suffered, both on the slave ships and later in the fields.

The Africans weren't the only ones to suffer under the European expansion of these times. La Rochelle's Museum of the New World reminded us, only too graphically, of the horrors inflicted on the indigenous populations of the West Indies and South America when Europeans invaded their lands and forced them into servitude on the new plantations. And when the natives died off through overwork and disease, the flourishing African trade filled the gap to keep the plantations going.

But human cruelty in Africa and the Americas wasn't confined to European perpetrators. Indigenous groups too, from Canada in the north to Peru in the south, inflicted their own atrocities on war captives and slaves, with ritual torture sometimes carried out even by women.

These museums reminded me of the Wars of Religion when Catholics and Protestants persecuted and massacred anyone who wavered from whatever the other side considered heretical. The St. Bartholomew's Day Massacre of 1572, which actually went on for around six weeks, was one of the worst with around thirty thousand Huguenots, or Protestants, slaughtered by frenzied mobs. This kind of persecution was finally brought to an end when the tolerant King Henry of Navarre signed the Edict of Nantes in 1598, guaranteeing Protestants some religious freedom, only for it to be revoked a century later, along with renewed repression.

And if that wasn't enough to take in, there was the French Revolution with its guillotine, and in Nantes, when that proved too slow, mass drownings in the River Loire. Then there was the daily misery of workers in the 19th century factories, with no rights to time off apart from church holidays, crushingly long hours, below-survival wages and filthy conditions.

Museums like those in Nantes and La Rochelle were stark reminders of humanity's dark side. Especially dangerous is mob fever when individuals, stirred by ritualistic chanting and relentless demagoguery, become a mindless dark force, unleashed to carry out all kinds of mindless cruelties. The rallies we've seen across the US, with crowds whipped up by simplistic slogans, brainless chants and mocking taunts, are frightening reminders of how this force has erupted in the past, like those Paris mobs screaming abuse at Marie Antoinette as her tumbril made its way to the Place de la Révolution and the guillotine.

But then there's the other side of the coin. Alongside the darkness of the human heart there's the light — and the never-ending battle between good and evil. In France alone, the chains of slavery have long since been banished, religious persecution is unthinkable and the daily grind of the workhouse has been replaced by the 30-hour week. But the psychological distance between those savage mobs of the past and the peaceful society of today is scarily short. The fragility of civilization — and the paradoxical nature of humankind — is something we must never forget.

However, it was the world of fairy tale, myth and legend that prevailed as we drove through Cristallin's gates for the last time and it was the questing legend of Parsifal that then seemed most apt. On our human journey we inevitably confront many choices and obstacles and if we're lucky, friends to guide and support us, just like Parsifal. To live the good life our choices must always be to suppress that dark side of human nature and nurture the good — to fight the good fight, despite the obstacles.

That was the story of our time at Cristallin too. It hadn't been easy dealing with the stinging nettles, blackberry thorns and rampant wisteria, knowing full well that even as we dug them out some roots remained, ready to invade once more without constant vigilance. Just like life.

12. Woods, Lakes and Leaves

They say that when one door closes another opens. It's also true of gates.

Hefting Cristallin's rusting gates, now cleared of ivy and brambles, and seeing them disappear in the rear-vision mirror had been a huge relief. Our three weeks in that dilapidated château had also at times been rather depressing and lonely. Apart from our afternoon with the Leblancs, we'd pretty well been on our own — quite a change from the UK where we had a wide network of friends and family.

So driving up to another forbidding iron gate at our next assignment didn't bode well. Neither did the house itself, again of solid stone and built over at least four floors. Shades of Cristallin! Its façade too, was somewhat forbidding. A broken wrought-iron railing lined steps leading to an imposing front door and, with windows on either side, it looked like a stern face glaring at us below.

But — surprise! The gate opened easily onto a tiny square drive surrounded by masses of pale yellow, heavily perfumed roses with not a blackberry stalk or ivy runner in sight. And then at the sound of our arrival Jan, the owner, and her two lively dogs, Scruff and Réglisse, appeared from behind the house to greet us.

Jan was a Welsh expat who had made a home for herself in the little village of Treignac, deep in the heart of this heavily wooded region of the Corrèze and deep in the heart of France, an area totally new to us. This has been another huge benefit of house sitting. We've stayed in places that we'd never heard of before and would never have chosen to visit on our own accord. House sitting has opened up a whole range of brand-new experiences, not to mention introducing us to new friends.

We started with a quick look around the garden, which was about as big as Cristallin's but spare and a bit dull rather than overgrown and wild. Jan later told us that it had once been a thriving market garden with vegetable beds and orchards long before she bought it, but gradually it had been turned into lawn when the previous owners grew too old to maintain it. Now it was a bit of a problem. It was too big to do anything imaginative that would need heaps of work but it was also a constant source of nagging anxiety. What to do with this lovely fertile piece of land that was more attractive but wouldn't need a whole lot of maintenance?

We kept telling ourselves that it was *her* problem but during our time there it also became ours as we wandered around its perimeter on evening dog walks, vainly trying to come up with a solution. It was a bit like the fruitless hours we spent at Cristallin thinking up renovation ideas for all those interconnecting bedrooms, tiny malfunctioning bathrooms and collapsing outbuildings.

Once inside the house though, we breathed a huge sigh of relief. What a difference a good layout makes to a home! Although originally divided into two halves by the front door, the ground floor was now mostly open plan with a comfortable sitting room, dining area and kitchen, all completely decorated in the Welsh national colours of red, white and green. Even her crockery, artwork, towels and bedding were in these colours with the odd ornamental dragon making an appearance now and then. It really did work though. This particular colour combination lent an overwhelming sense of cheerfulness but also of calm. The deep greens were soothing, the reds energizing and the whites provided breathing space.

The décor was a mirror image of Jan herself. That evening she welcomed us with a lovely dinner as a way of meeting her friends, both French and expat. She'd prepared heaps of delicious food creatively laid out on red, white and green platters and had set up a table on the outside terrace that was framed with climbing roses. How she managed to do all that cooking, clearing up and then get organized to head off the next morning was a mystery. But she did it — calmly and amiably.

Only one thing spoiled this otherwise splendid welcome and that was when we saw our bedroom. As we climbed the staircases going from the living area to the first floor guest rooms and then up the narrower staircase to our room under the eaves, memories of the Cristallin attic began creeping back. But the warm reds and greens of the duvet and the adjoining modern white bathroom put my mind at ease. That is until I saw, in each corner of the room, a large comfy dog bed.

Jan, being the open and friendly person that she was, happily admitted that she herself wasn't keen on this arrangement. It was, she said, all the fault of her former partner but now the two dogs were in the habit of sleeping up there, it seemed too hard to get them to change. But change they would, if we were to get any sleep!

Scruff and Réglisse were very different dogs in both nature and appearance. Scruff was a light-coloured, wiry-haired rescue dog, saved by Jan from his precarious existence on the streets of Cardiff. He was well behaved —

unexpected in a dog that had roamed homeless for heaven knows how long — very endearing and very canny. Réglisse, or liquorice, was a French dog, a lot feistier and a bit of a struggle when on the lead, straining after other dogs, horses and whatever interesting sight or smell took her fancy.

Both dogs stayed downstairs with Jan that night before she left for the airport. But the next evening as we headed upstairs for bed and they immediately jumped up from their downstairs' cushions to pad up beside us, we knew we had trouble. So we took them back downstairs, settled them in the sitting room and shut the hallway door firmly behind us. A little later, just as we were nodding off, we heard snuffling sounds — and there they were. They'd somehow managed to open the hallway door and sneak upstairs without us hearing a sound.

After a few more attempts to return them downstairs and with them reappearing each time, Richard discovered that it was Scruff with his finely honed door-opening skills acquired from his life on the streets that was the breaking-and-entering expert. Every night from then on, after settling them downstairs, we'd go through the ritual of barring the door and propping up the handle with mops and brooms. Problem solved.

We'd been pleasantly surprised when driving along the winding road to Treignac to see so many deep valleys, lakes and thick forests with relatively few villages. Both the natural and built environments in this area were stunning. However, as we explored the village and beyond, we couldn't help but notice the number of vacant or derelict properties, especially in the smaller towns and in villages like Treignac. On the other hand, bigger towns such as Angoulême, Brive and Tulle were vibrant with plenty of restaurants, bars and shops. These towns had the best of both worlds — some of the loveliest, simplest old Romanesque churches we'd seen, as well as dynamic activity. The countryside seemed to be emptying and the bigger towns expanding.

The village was lovely with its old stone buildings, winding roads, little squares and rushing river cutting through the deep valley. But we definitely felt a sense of mild gloom, which I put down to the shape of the valley itself. We loved our walks up through the woods near the house to the rugged cliffs overlooking the gorge but the village itself was at the bottom, divided by the bridge. As picturesque and dramatic as the setting was, the hard reality is that with deep valleys come dark shadows, chilly early sunsets and late sunrises.

Still, we thoroughly enjoyed our dog sit in Treignac. It had been a place of rest and repose, very welcome after the nettles of Cristallin. We'd have morning coffee sitting outside a café near the bridge, dogs tethered to table legs, and would enjoy chatting with the café owners. Then there were villagers we'd meet while out walking as well as Jan's friends who'd drop by the house to see how we were doing. It certainly wouldn't be too hard fitting into a place like this. Apart from the early afternoon shadows, it was easy to see the attraction.

Despite the population shrinkage though, there was still plenty of life in the village and a bit of whimsy as well.

One weekend we were thrilled to discover a festival being held that included a weird homemade billy cart race down one of the village's steepest streets, accompanied by Brazilian music. And one day while out walking the dogs, we were surprised by a multi-coloured, larger-than-life cow sculpture on the front lawn of a remote hillside house. Not at all traditionally French but quite fitting in this good-natured, fun-loving village.

For eating out, we'd head to the more open lakes and restaurants with sunny terraces that some of our new expat acquaintances had recommended. They too were thinking of moving on but more as a result of the uncertainty surrounding the Brexit vote than discontent with the village itself. The results of the referendum had come as a huge shock to all. With such a slim majority voting to leave the European Union and knowing from our time in the UK how torn so many people were, it was clear this wouldn't be an easy result to live with.

The morning after the referendum we went to the café for our usual morning coffee, a bit worried as to the reaction of the locals there, but to our relief, all was calm. Some even said they could understand and sympathize with the vote. Our expat acquaintances, shocked, depressed and concerned about the future, were also reluctant to criticise. Their main worry was whether they'd be allowed to stay in France and if they'd have to take a language test or whether they'd be better off heading to Spain where they had a better grasp of the language — and where it was warmer.

At that moment though, with the vote to leave the EU, Prime Minister David Cameron's subsequent resignation, a horrible political murder in the UK and a mass shooting in Florida, Treignac seemed an island of sanity and calm amidst chaos and confusion.

Our last lunch was on the sunny veranda of our favourite restaurant beside the lake at Seilhac, where we'd become regulars and were warmly welcomed. When we finally had to leave, it was with fond memories of kindly people, a lush landscape and a leisurely but warmly communal way of life.

Whenever we travelled through France, we'd stop for a couple of days to visit our friends, clarinettist Mervyn and his French wife Catherine, who had a rambling house, La Source, on the outskirts of Casteljaloux in the Lot-et-Garonne area. Casteljaloux is a lively town near a lake and has a bit of everything — water sports, a golf club and thermal baths, as well as the more traditional draw cards such as picturesque old streets and bi-weekly farmers' markets.

We'd first met when we all lived near Washington D.C. where Mervyn often performed in the concert hall in nearby Old Town, Alexandria. They moved back to London shortly after we did so we saw quite a bit of them.

Late in the winter while we were still living in Chipping Campden we'd stayed with Mervyn in their London flat for a few days while Catherine was in France preparing their house for sale. They'd spent many wonderful summers there with their extended families visiting from the UK and the US but sadly, it was time to let it go. Mervyn, now in his eighties, had been diagnosed with dementia and so making the journey to Casteljaloux was becoming just too difficult.

Catherine had arranged for a carer to stay with Mervyn on the weekday afternoons so we were able to go out for a few hours each day. We were keen to visit the Wellcome Collection, a museum dedicated to just about anything concerning medical science — art, models, artefacts — and it was supposed to have a superb library and reading room. It certainly didn't disappoint. Housed in a refurbished London building with contemporary light-filled open spaces and a luxuriously appointed reading room with ample seating — colourful sofas, bean bags and artisan chairs — it was a gem.

One temporary exhibit that really piqued our interest was called *States of Mind: Tracing the Edges of Consciousness*, which delved into the great existential questions: What is consciousness? What is the mind? Is the mind separate from the body? Just about every mind experiment I'd ever read about was on display here, covering unconsciousness, hypnotism, sleep, memory and much more.

Having spent a fair bit of time now with Mervyn, this subject seemed more fascinating than ever. When memories start dissolving and language fails, who and where is the 'real' person? And what is a 'real' person anyway? Does the 'I' actually exist? What makes us — us? Such questions inevitably arise when you see someone living with dementia.

Knowing a person in his prime and then witnessing this kind of mental dissolution is very hard. His personality was still intact though — as gentlemanly and sweet as ever, and he'd not lost his abiding love of music.

When we joined Catherine and Mervyn at La Source where they were enjoying one last summer, we found Mervyn to be the same smiling, courteous, generous host as before, always alert to see if he could offer a bit more pâté or a drinks top-up, though occasionally confusing coffee mugs with liqueur glasses. Being served a huge slug of port could be a bit daunting early in the day, whether in Portugal or in France. Although he no longer played the clarinet, he spent his days listening to music and reading from the bundle of music scores that rarely left his side.

A conversation with Mervyn was a bit like an abstract painting. The key words were there and they reflected his sophisticated vocabulary. But their arrangement, the syntax, was muddled and mixed in kaleidoscope patterns that hinted at meaning but which mostly eluded both parties. Music was a common feature of this 'Mervlish' idiolect. He described the sound of the stream running through their garden as 'chamber music'; the large-leaved plants growing from its banks were 'French horns or trumpets'. He loved sharing his scores and would describe each musical phrase using language of action — how 'something's going on here' or 'a change is happening now' — visibly excited as he heard the music in his mind.

Catherine had created a comfortable, harmonious home full of fascinating books and memorabilia of their life together with most rooms opening onto the cool, scented garden with its ferny *source* running beneath the dining room windows. We spent lazy days meeting Catherine's friends, cooking, chatting and eating beneath the garden's shady trees. Suffice it to say that Franglais, French and English flowed fairly easily, with plenty of Mervlish to keep us on our toes.

The only time during our stay when we literally hit a brick wall was when Richard slammed our car into a low barrier as he was pulling out from the pavement beside the house. We didn't notice the damage until we stopped in the town car park and stood horrified, watching as coolant flooded out from the car's underbelly. To add insult to injury, a passer-by, obviously furious at the Brexit result and hearing us speaking in English, let out a stream of abuse of the 'Go home Brit!' variety, adding a frisson of foreboding while we awaited the tow truck. This vote to leave the EU wasn't received with as much equanimity as we'd first thought back in Treignac. But with Richard being an American and me being (mostly) an Australian, it was even funny in a grim sort of way.

The highlight of our stay was the farewell dinner the night before we were to leave for Spain. Catherine had invited her French friends to join us, not only for us all to say goodbye but also because Mervyn loved company.

He also loved wine, another personality trait that had not deserted him, and that was tricky when trying to limit his intake. Our guests had brought along a couple of bottles of French red but with all the excitement and distraction of entertaining, trying to keep these hidden from him was virtually useless — his wine-seeking radar was exceptionally well honed. Mervyn was in his element.

How much happier could anyone be? To sit laughing and chatting with friends old and new (even if a muddle of English, French and Mervlish) around a simple candlelit table, eating a lovingly prepared meal with the garden darkening and the *source* bubbling outside — this could not be trumped, no matter how many golden escalators or crystal chandeliers you owned.

And the *pièce de résistance*?

As we all rose from the table to say our goodbyes, Catherine, on the spur of the moment, embraced us all in a warm group hug. And to our shock and surprise, Mervyn suddenly underwent a metamorphosis. No longer the dementia sufferer, he became the maestro of old. He commanded his audience. He spoke of love, friendship and happiness. In that moment, Mervyn the conductor, musician, teacher and friend was manifest once more. He had not entirely left us. His ability to inspire and delight was still there.

So with warm hearts we prepared to leave La Source and Casteljaloux for the last time — and sadly it was also the last time we were to see Mervyn, as he passed away a few months later.

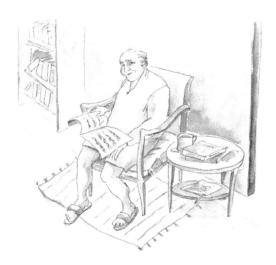

AMONG THE
OLIVE GROVES

13. Heat, Dust and Blasts from the Past

Another country, another pet sit and another gate. On our four-day journey from Casteljaloux we'd driven from the lush, cool Pyrenees through a tunnel to emerge in the parched, searing landscape of Spain.

The directions sent by Sylvia and David on how to find their house were extremely detailed and precise, for which we were truly grateful. Our GPS was certainly not up to the task of negotiating this confusing network of country roads with its string of hamlets so tiny you'd miss them if you blinked. Fortunately we just managed to catch a glimpse of the signpost to Las Grajeras, which was to be our closest hamlet, and a bit further on found what hoped was the 'Social', a tiny but well-maintained building where, as Sylvia and David later told us, a fiesta would be held the following night.

Hoping for the best, we turned off and bumped down a dirt lane past endless olive groves, gratefully finding that the last of the directions were spot on: 'A white house with black gates and one black dog.'

The heavy iron gates opened onto a Spanish version of heaven, heralded by the excited barks of one black, though slightly dusty dog. David and Sylvia had transformed this previously dilapidated, rabbit warren of a house, once surrounded by barren earth, into their own piece of paradise. The whitewashed villa with its blue shutters and little shady balconies stood proudly alone atop a hill and had panoramic views over endless olive groves to the craggy mountains beyond. Yes, the name Las Colinas was perfect.

Off to the side was a plunge pool with a shady outdoor dining area decorated with pots of hot pink geraniums. Other more intimate sitting spots were tucked away throughout the terraced gardens that merged into the olive groves below. One that became a favourite was a little sunken terrace with a Moorish blue and white tiled fountain, complete with fish. Apart from the natural sounds of chooks and the odd barking dog, this was a level of peace and quiet that we hadn't experienced in a very long time and was especially welcome after all those clanging bells at Cristallin.

On our first night Sylvia and David took us to the closest big town, Alcalá la Real, to try some tapas and the fabulous local red wine. At eight when we arrived, the town was deceptively quiet. But by nine it was buzzing and it was pumping at ten. And that was just in the local park. Kids, grandmothers, old men and young couples — everyone was out having fun. Even the roundabout heading into town with its whimsical industrial scrap and tile sculptures was fun.

As for the pets, Spain looked like being a winner, what with two self-sufficient cats, one who made herself at home on Rick's stomach as he lay resting on the terrace on the first day, and the endearing, well-behaved black Labrador, Rossi.

He *was* a bit naughty on our first day and we feared we had a rebel on our hands. Sylvia and David had told us that he was absolutely allowed in one room only, the little TV room between the outside door and the kitchen, and he'd certainly obeyed when they were around. But within hours of them leaving, he'd followed us into the kitchen and simply refused to budge from beneath the breakfast counter.

Sylvia and David hadn't been joking when they warned us about possible noise from the fiesta as they headed off to begin their campervan holiday. We'd imagined it would be an evening affair. But no. It started in the afternoon and continued well into the night with plenty of fireworks and loud singing that echoed clearly across all those hills. Remembering Tilly the cat's fear of fireworks on New Year's Eve in Leiden, we wondered if the same applied to Rossi, what with all the fiesta celebrations and noisy rocket firing.

And so it was. After a few more fruitless attempts at shoving his immobile black bulk back through the doorway, we relented and let him stay with us in the kitchen. The next day when the fiesta was over and the rockets had all been fired, Rossi returned to his normal well-behaved self, lying on the TV room tiles, nose between paws *just* hanging down over the kitchen step, and there he stayed.

Spain is hot. Very hot and very dry. A fine layer of dust from the olive groves and the dirt road that ran beside the house gradually settled over everything — our car, the tiled floors and Rossi. But at dusk the heavy perfume of roses and lilies, the cool breeze and apricot sky, made enduring the daytime heat worthwhile.

We tried living like Spaniards, which wasn't too hard because the temperature simply dictated it. Early morning was for plant watering, animal feeding, dog walking and general chores. Later in the morning was coffee time, either under the bamboo pergola beside the pool while it was still in shade or wherever we happened to be if out for the day — a *cortado* for me and a *café solo* for Richard. Thank heavens we had a few essential Spanish words and phrases up our sleeves. The Park café in town offered a good two-euro deal for coffee and *churros*, Spain's delicate, lighter variation on the American doughnut, and scarily addictive. Fortunately though, it was the kind of treat that tastes best in its country of origin, along with Pimm's in England and Mai Tais in Hawaii, so this addiction didn't follow us once we left Spain.

After lunch it was a museum or gallery visit, or perhaps a hot stroll through one of the pretty towns nearby, keeping to the shady side of the street. Early evenings were dedicated to walks with Rossi through the bone-dry olive groves with all of us, not just Rossi, coming back home dry, dusty and very hot.

One such evening's outing was cut short when Rossi suddenly bolted and returned with a huge, square, rubbery object firmly clasped in his jaws. We didn't have a clue what it was but it looked horribly like a chunk of animal hide. Because he'd immediately taken off again into the dust, not to reappear for an *unusually* long time, even though he normally stuck to us like glue — and minus the mystery object — we could only imagine he'd buried it somewhere for his later delectation. Sylvia had said he sometimes turned up with the odd goat's leg but this suspicious behaviour led us to believe it was something forbidden and totally ghastly. It was better not to know.

After the evening walk, followed by a quick sluice to wash off the worst of the dust, we would begin our dinner preparations. This was usually a small barbeque of sardines or lamb chops with salad, cooked and eaten outside with a glass of chilled rosé, at our favourite time of day when the sun was slowly sinking behind the hills. Rossi would sit with us till around ten, when he'd quietly lope off to his bed in the outhouse with the two no-nonsense, no-frills cats already settled in the top bunk.

There were so many things to love about this country. One was the care lavished on parks, balconies and courtyard gardens. If there was no space for a garden, there would be plants in pots — hanging on walls, from balcony railings and lining steps.

Another was that joyful sense of community we'd seen firsthand with the fiesta at the Social and in Alcalá la Real on our first evening. Every morning in the park near the café, we'd see rows of neatly dressed elderly men sitting on a low wall chatting and passing the time of day. A few years earlier when a car park had been built beneath the park, its entrance had cut through part of the wall, breaking its continuity. But much to our amusement, the local government had decorated the side of the car park with a life-sized mural of the men who used to sit there when that bit of wall existed.

I wondered though how a country with such strong social bonds had managed to heal itself after the civil war when families and villagers were torn apart, supporting or even fighting on opposing sides. Those old men would probably have been small children back then, so time seemed somehow to have done its work. Where all their wives were I had no idea, though maybe in this seemingly macho culture, they were at home getting lunch ready or watering all those pot plants.

Spanish history is pretty grim, what with the Inquisition, the barbarity of the conquistadors in the New World and more recently, the civil war. I confess that I knew very little about this part of Spanish history and what I did know was from reading Ernest Hemingway's *For Whom the Bell Tolls* at college. I was so glad that I'd brought along another novel set in that era, *The Return* by Victoria Hislop. This is a time-slip novel switching between present day Granada and the civil war of the '30s and it proved to be an entertaining and digestible way of discovering some background. Literature allows us to immerse ourselves in another time or place and even when somewhat factually flawed, can provide us with an imaginative landscape, as well as the motivation to learn more.

It's also much easier and more gripping learning about the history of a place when you're actually there on the spot and that applies whether you're visiting stately homes, cities or entire countries. For example, in Spain we could view artworks such as Picasso's *Guernica* painted as a response to the civil war and Goya's *Disasters of War* depicting the horrors of the 1808 French invasion, as well as visit the actual towns, villages and cities where these events took place.

But what I found truly unsettling was learning how the Church had been so complicit in supporting the fascist forces. It was hard to believe that the pope actually sent Franco a letter of congratulation when he conquered Madrid. Knowing how widespread and widely reported were the horrors unleashed by the civil war, the part played by the Church was even more depressing.

When Richard and I first met and were hanging out in Calella on the Costa Brava for a few days in 1972, we were both completely oblivious to all this history and even to the fact that Spain was still a dictatorship controlled by Franco so many years after the civil war. Our main concern then was the Vietnam War, which was the reason for Richard even being in Europe at that time, having been forced by the draft to cut his studies short and enlist in the military. Spanish politics wasn't even on the radar. But also we were young, a long way from home, having adventures — and we were pretty naive.

It was the time of flower power, hippies and the counter-culture.

One novel that had not only piqued my interest in Spain as a travel destination but also in the world of the counter-culture, especially in its American guise, was James Michener's *The Drifters*. Perhaps it was this book more than any other that had lured me from the safety — and boredom — of my job in suburban Sydney to head off backpacking around Europe in search of adventures, which I secretly but unrealistically hoped would be as transformational as those experienced by Michener's characters.

So when we were driving from Las Colinas to Malaga one day and I saw a sign to Torremolinos, one of the most alluring locations in *The Drifters*, all that carefree early '70s optimism came flooding back. Those were the days — before the grimness of grunge, Mohawk haircuts and safety pin earrings, and when smiles, not scowls, were in. We were fashion conscious but in the free-and-easy way of Indian cotton midriff tops, flower-embroidered bell bottoms and cork-soled platform shoes, all of which still seemed to be on offer in many of Malaga's tourist shops.

The Spanish themselves though, seemed fairly dismissive of all that counter-culture, new-age stuff, except for selling it to tourists. They did their own fabulous Spanish thing with swirly skirts, frills and striking colour schemes — not so much laid-back or Indian-inspired 'spiritual' but vivacious, cheeky and heart warming.

We were in Granada one Saturday and by chance found ourselves in the middle of some kind of huge fiesta. At the head of the procession was an ornate, flower-encrusted carriage bearing an impressive silvery Madonna, followed by ladies and gents on horseback in full Spanish kit but with wildly idiosyncratic colour schemes. Then came more carriages; a herd of cattle, which seemed a bit odd; and finally a bunch of well-dressed, well-mannered children. We had no idea what it was all about but my guess was Corpus Christi, though the inclusion of the herd of cattle was puzzling.

Just as we'd managed to extricate ourselves from that jolly scene, we ran into a wedding with another well-dressed crowd, singing and clapping, decked out in their best Spanish finery of feathery hats, glittery shoes, polka dots and frills, cheering the newlyweds as they emerged from the church to climb into a vintage car awaiting them in the square.

But what happened as the wedding party dispersed was equally intriguing. About ten minutes after the newlyweds' departure, much to our surprise, we discovered all six bridesmaids, unmissable in their cobalt-blue dresses, matching stilettoes and scarlet floral hair clips, standing around an upside-down keg at a nearby bar having a glass of *tinto de verano*. Was this how a Spanish wedding ends, not with a bang but with a glass of summer wine?

This scene brought back memories of a trip to Seville a few years earlier when, in search of a particular church with the famous Virgin of Macarena, we entered what we hoped was the church in question, only to find ourselves trapped in the middle of a mass christening service with no Macarena — or exit route — in sight.

A never-ending stream of babies was being carried up to the font to be christened and we were starting to wonder if we'd ever be able to escape. It was only when the priest finally reached the group-handshaking part of the service that we managed to beat a hasty retreat to what seemed an escape route through a set of doors on the far side of the church. No such luck. These doors opened onto another room with even more doors leading to heaven knows where.

Returning to the mass christening wasn't an option so we took a punt and opened one likely-looking door, only to find ourselves literally face-to-face with another massive congregation, this time minus babies but with hundreds of flamboyant mantilla- and polka-dot-bedecked ladies and wide-brimmed, black-hat-wearing men.

We stood frozen for a few seconds in the doorway, which we only then realized was directly beside the altar and so in full view, when suddenly the whole congregation stood up and began surging towards us. This was our chance to escape and we took it, pushing through the crowd and heading out the front church door into the darkening square.

As we looked back into the brightly lit church, we realized we'd crashed a wedding in the very church we'd been trying to find. There above the altar was the Macarena — a giant, silvery Kewpie doll of a statue towering over the happy couple. She was certainly impressive and well worth the effort of trying to find her. Unfortunately though, we weren't going to be joining in any of the post-wedding celebrations that, by the look of those flamboyant outfits, were bound to be great fun. Though on retrospect, we'd probably have found it all happening around some upside-down beer kegs down in the square.

We were sad to leave the lovely Las Colinas but David and Sylvia ensured we had a grand send-off. The night they returned, they took us to a tapas bar in Almedinilla, a 'white village' about halfway between Las Grajeras and Priego.

So there we were, in the middle of olive groves in a tiny village on a slow Monday night, enjoying unexpectedly fabulous mojitos and tapas. The owner, a non-English speaker, had picked up bits of our conversation about the Eric Clapton concert Sylvia and David had recently been to in London, and how terribly seasick they'd been on the ferry crossing. This led to me telling the tale of my first trip to the UK on the Greek liner *Australis* and the disco nights we spent dancing to Credence Clearwater Revival's 'Proud Mary' while the ship too, rocked and rolled.

A few minutes later, we noticed the owner busily erecting speakers outside the restaurant door. Then all became clear as Credence's 'Suzie Q' filled the previously whisper-quiet square.

It seemed that he was mad about music from the '70s and was only too happy to grab the chance of sharing his passion with kindred spirits. So as he worked his way through his collection of Eric Clapton, Pink Floyd and Jefferson Airplane CDs, we felt duty bound to order another round of mojitos before taking our leave.

The next day we said our goodbyes to sad, dusty Rossi, still amused that the highlight of our ten-day stay, already so full of highlights, was the night we were entertained, not by flamenco dancers or gypsy guitarists in a smoke-filled tavern, but by a Spanish soft rock aficionado with an impressive CD collection in a tiny village in the middle of olive groves.

14. Casa de Gatos

Stephen Hawking famously wrote that the world faces two main problems: pollution and stupidity. With all the turmoil in the world, much of it self-inflicted, I'd give Hawking top marks for pithy accuracy.

So far that year in the UK alone we'd had the shock result of the Brexit referendum rapidly followed by Prime Minister David Cameron's resignation. Then there was the release of the damming Chilcot report into the Iraq War, even more rapidly followed by images of Tony Blair's haggard visage and public shaming.

In Europe there'd been the Bastille Day slaughter in Nice, an attempted coup in Turkey and hot on the heels of that, the roundup of thousands of alleged coup-plotters, which the Turkish government managed to discover suspiciously quickly.

In the US it was the Pulse nightclub mass shooting and Donald Trump sounding more every day like something straight from the pages of George Orwell's dystopian fictions, *Animal Farm* or *1984*.

And as for pollution, scientists reported the worst mangrove die-off ever recorded in the Gulf of Carpentaria, the worst bleaching event ever on the Great Barrier Reef that had killed off a quarter of the coral, and the wiping out of 100km of kelp forest in Western Australia. All of this was the result of warming water, caused by our polluting greenhouse gases. And that was just in Australia.

When it comes down to it, stupidity — or to put it more generously, ignorance — was the prime mover behind so many of these tragedies. Ignorant people don't understand science: the properties of gases, the carbon cycle, the difference between climate and weather. They don't understand psychology or logic so rarely analyse the soundness of claims made on their Twitter feeds or TV screens. Ignorant people are easily manipulated by unscrupulous politicians and snake-oil salesmen who know how to stroke egos and stoke hateful emotions in mass rallies with their repetitive chants, mindless slogans and empty promises.

On the plus side, the space probe *Juno* entered mighty Jupiter's orbit taking us on the next step of humankind's adventure in space, Barack Obama banned gas and oil drilling in the Arctic, and a zero-fuel plane circumnavigated the globe. Hopefully none of these were stupid, with the last two being notable for their pollution-mitigating rationales.

While on the road in Spain heading to our different pet-sitting assignments, we made a point of stopping off at places where we'd never been before. Two cities that brought into sharp relief this dichotomy in human nature, the dark versus the light, were the inland city of Zaragoza in the north and the port city of Valencia in the east.

The Goya museum in Zaragoza confronted us with room after room of Goya's images of the misery and mayhem he witnessed two centuries ago in Spain. His stark etchings of the Inquisition, war and the madhouse — the *casa de locos* — took no prisoners, literally or metaphorically. The ease with which humans could descend into brutish cruelty was depicted simply and truthfully. No explanation was needed: the images said it all. Here, laid bare, was the horrifying reality of all that writers like George Orwell warn of in their dystopian fictions.

The cathedral too, spoke volumes about the doublethink that is essential for bolstering any autocratic regime, be it religious or secular. In Spain this was manifested in the deep religious conviction underpinning mass torture — the mercy of Christ demanding salvation through rack and pyre. Unlike the peaceful simplicity of the Romanesque churches we'd visited in towns around Treignac, the cathedral in Zaragoza had been designed to impress and overwhelm — both mind and senses. It was hard to reconcile a mindset that could create such beauty while also accepting the torments of the torture chamber.

I wondered too, how the design of such buildings, whether simple or ornate, might impact the human psyche. For me, simpler churches allow room for contemplation and the space to look within, as with that Cotswold Quaker meetinghouse, while majestic, ornate cathedrals force my attention outwards. They are awe-inspiring but can also be intimidating.

So feeling slightly queasy from Goya's hellish visions and the deep questions inspired by Zaragoza's cathedral, we hit the road and headed to Valencia. We left our car at a small hotel in what turned out to be the Red Light district and followed a long, hot but promising trail through parkland to the Promised Land: the City of Arts and Sciences. What a change! Superstition vanquished by science and the ascent of reason. Well, Goya gave up on that concept but Galileo *did* eventually win out over the Inquisition, even if not in his lifetime. So on we humans go, in fits and starts.

What an exhilarating monument this was to the best in humankind with its soaring architecture and clear palette of whites, blues and pale greens. Rising from vast pools of water were the shimmering gold pillars of Heinz Mack's majestic installation, *The Sky Over Nine Columns*, reminding me of those eerie monoliths in Stanley Kubrick's film *2001 A Space Odyssey* but without the solemnity. There was an overwhelming sense of optimism for the human project, something we sorely needed at that point.

A building designed along these lines would create the perfect place for contemplation by combining the best of both worlds — a vast yet simple space inspiring both tranquillity as well as awe. I could imagine being encompassed by the comforting curves of such clean simple lines while being uplifted by the soaring sweep of clear blues, greens and golds.

So, on to our next Spanish pet sit, once more in the Andalusian countryside but this time on the outskirts of the medium-sized hill town, Alhaurín el Grande. Where our previous sit had been totally secluded with nothing but olive groves as far as the eye could see, here we were part of a small farming community with neighbours on every side — not exactly on our doorstep, but certainly within eye- and ear-shot.

The house opened directly onto a narrow road and sat on a pie-shaped piece of land with an extensive garden out back. The living room flowed to a veranda decorated with Balinese mirrors and rustic candles and furnished with wooden-framed sofas made comfortable with white cotton throws and colourful cushions. Wisteria wound up to the roof and masses of succulents framed the tiled floor and little circle of lawn beyond. A winding stone path led down through shrubs and trees to a long wooden table in the BBQ area and the orchard beyond. These outside areas were so inviting that we spent most afternoons relaxing on the veranda or cooking down at the BBQ spot after returning from our day's explorations.

The house itself was simple and easy to take care of with its open-plan ground floor designed for cooking, eating and lounging and just two bedrooms and a bathroom upstairs.

The pets were two very sweet dogs, Laura and Dixie, and two amiable cats, Sammy and Zorro — two pets more than we were comfortable with at that stage, but since we'd committed to this sit quite a while ago, we couldn't let the family down. They'd been very kind, even preparing a lovely surprise dinner of paella and cake to celebrate my birthday the night we arrived. Sitting by candlelight under the bamboo pergola at the BBQ spot, sharing a lovingly prepared Spanish meal with this Dutch family boded well for our stay.

But kind as they were, we soon began wondering if kindness could at times be somewhat misplaced. What we had not expected was the number of strays that they'd taken on and that we were now responsible for feeding twice a day, along with extensive garden watering and all the 'normal' pet duties like dog walking, feeding and general companionship.

The strays hung out in the patio right off the kitchen and on the kitchen window ledge. This patio must once have been a pretty little area with pot plants hanging on the walls as with so many Spanish houses but it was now a desolate, no-go area. The cats could get through the fence into the orchard next door with its goats, dogs and fruit trees but they tended to stay in the patio, hanging about the kitchen door waiting for food so it somewhat resembled a prison exercise area. It wasn't as if they even looked happy or healthy. Even though fed twice a day, somehow they were still mangy, thin and scrawny.

To stop them coming into the house, the owners had installed a barred door so what with that, plus the glass door that we couldn't open more than a crack in case they squeezed through, and all the food bowls lining the door step, trying to cross the patio to reach the storage shed was like storming a barricade. As for letting the cool breeze blow through, forget it. The only thing that would have blown through would have been an army of feral cats. Even washing up at the kitchen sink felt like being under threat of invasion with more cats crouched between the window glass and security bars, scrutinizing every movement.

The kitchen cupboards and outside storage shed were full of pet food. There were pet beds and mats on every piece of furniture, including the dining table, and in every room except our bedroom — thank heavens — but even so there were four pet beds on the landing right outside the bedroom door.

It did make us wonder. We both love animals but after living with all those strays for a couple of weeks, if it had been up to us, we'd have had them humanely put down and donated the money saved from buying all that cat food to an endangered species charity! Luckily the cats couldn't read our minds and strangely seemed to like being around us, even when food wasn't involved.

Take our daily walks. At first we were just taking dogs Dixie and Laura for their morning walk down the road past more orchards and clumps of sugarcane. Then one morning we found we had an extra animal with us — Sammy, one of the house cats. The next day Zorro, the more elusive house cat, leapt over the wall as we walked past and he too joined our animal parade. And a couple of days after that, we had all four pets plus one of the stray cats for the entirety of the walk. I could feel my heart start to soften.

But apart from all these animal and garden duties, we were pleased to have the chance to spend more time in this part of Spain, which is so interesting and beautiful but also quite challenging. The heat and humidity were dreadful and we were disturbed to see so many invasive plants taking over extensive parts of the landscape. But wherever the native pine tree cover was intact, it was quite lovely.

Much of the architecture was a clever marriage of form and function with thick white walls, shady pathways between the houses and plant-filled patios adding interest as well as welcome outdoor space. Spending time in these lovely white villages brought home how human-scale, beautiful architecture with gardens and outdoor spaces treasured and lovingly cared for by their residents can raise the general happiness level to a degree city planners and developers don't often appreciate.

Because of the heat we kept to short walks interspersed with coffee breaks and lunches and best of all, some moseying around in the area's wonderful art galleries. The Picasso Museum in Malaga was a favourite and although I was glad we'd seen the Goya Museum, I must admit to enjoying a bit of light relief. Picasso's art, at least in that particular gallery, was just so much more cheerful than the horrors depicted by Goya. Maybe I needed to take a break from watching the news as well.

The colour red too joined the list of things I was starting to love about Spain: red cherries, tomatoes, peppers, watermelon, roses, geraniums — and garlic prawns.

Back in the late '60s my friends and I had discovered a very popular, somewhat edgy restaurant called Amado's Spanish Fiesta in Sydney's seedy Kings Cross area. It was located in a dungeon-like basement of indeterminate size, as you couldn't see from one end to the other through the thick fog of cigarette smoke. But I will never forget that small stage in the middle of the room; the stamping, shouting flamenco dancers; the polka-dot skirts and the sizzling ramekins of bright red garlic prawns.

So one day in Malaga when I saw a menu board with a photo of those same brown earthenware ramekins filled with the same spicy, aromatic prawns, I knew where we'd be having lunch that day and we were not disappointed.

All too soon it was time to take our leave of Andalusia and make our way north through the Basque area, the Pyrenees and then up the Atlantic coast of France to Caen.

We'd left our *casa de gatos*, which often seemed more like Goya's *casa de locos* as we forced our way through the barred kitchen doors and past the howling cats massed in the patio, swearing never again to take on more than two pets at a time.

Our time on the Costa del Sol had left us with mixed feelings. The inland areas with their endless olive groves, white villages, vivid red flowers and blue pottery were stunning. The beaches though, with their greyish sand and sweaty sunbathers stretched cheek to jowl were quite the opposite. But that wasn't what we'd gone there for. After all, we were from Sydney and Florida. Why go to Spain for its beaches? We were there to soak in the soul of Spain and that was to be found inland — in the smaller villages like Almedinilla and regional towns like Alcalá la Real and Alhaurín el Grande.

Heading north through high sierras, a very different landscape greeted us. Instead of dry, dusty hills and baking, grey sand, we were now buffeted by cold winds as we drove though forests, past dramatic rock formations and with *water* — so much fresh water — in rivers, waterfalls and dams. On previous trips to Spain we'd been to the big cities of Madrid, Seville and Barcelona. We'd never visited this part of the country with its powerful landscapes and forbidding, dark-timbered houses, so different from the dry heat and lighter colours of the south. What if the Spaniards rather than the English had been the ones to settle Australia in the 1700s, I wondered? The architecture might have been better for a start.

The Spaniards certainly knew how to build for both searing heat and biting cold.

The only thing that spoiled this amazing drive was a worrying rattling noise from the centre panel of the car. After driving for hours with the growing realisation that something was really wrong and imagining breaking down in the middle of nowhere in the freezing cold with no real grasp of Spanish, apart from being able to order coffee and churros, we gratefully pulled into a Mercedes Benz place that miraculously appeared on the road into Logroño.

Thanks to my *Get By In Spanish* book, we managed to explain the problem to the friendly servicemen who found, after spending an hour investigating, that a broken clip had caused some cable or other to touch the axle. So it wasn't the disc pads wearing down or anything really serious, as we'd feared.

How much for an hour's work?

Nada — niente — rien. Absolutely zip. Another tip of the hat to Spain and its people. Thoughts of Goya's etchings and all those wailing *gatos* were fading fast.

Logroño — Rioja and tapas.

What a great town, with its old quarter full of buzzing tapas bars and its newer wide boulevards with their idiosyncratic roundabouts, some like miniature woods, gardens and art installations. After browsing the many tapas bars, we finally settled on one where other diners helped us interpret the menu. With asparagus, red peppers, strawberries and a great Rioja coming our way, eating on the 'tapas trail' was the perfect conclusion to a very busy day.

I'd been wondering why the unexpected seemed to have dominated so much of this trip. But sitting there in this friendly tapas bar in Logroño, I suddenly nailed it. By organizing our trip around places that just 'came' to us from house-sitting listings, we'd been blown about by the whims of chance, more so than if we'd followed a more conventional itinerary with greater predictability. There'd been some scary moments but it had been well worth it.

We would never have done this drive through the Basque country seeing all those dripping forests, misty peaks, rushing streams and dark-timbered, red-shuttered houses if it hadn't been for pet sitting at Alhaurín el Grande.

And we probably wouldn't have broken the drive to France the following day in Hondarribia, another Basque town and also the scene of our last Spanish adventure. As we strolled around the old part of town looking for somewhere to have dinner, we came across a very strange sight. At first I thought we'd been caught up in some sort of ETA coup, with soldiers running down the street and an old Mercedes and Citroën standing by as likely get-away vehicles — until we saw the film crew.

Once again we'd landed in the middle of a film shoot.

So *adios* Spain and *bonjour* France. We hadn't been expecting any surprises here as we made our way up the coast to the ferry port but again, the great disrupter — fate — stepped in.

I'd booked somewhere to stay overnight at a place called Château Châtenay, which looked nice enough on their website but as booking sight unseen is always a bit hit and miss, we tend to keep our expectations fairly low.

Quelle surprise! It was as if we'd suddenly been transported back to Cristallin but after a fairy godmother had waved her magic wand. Suddenly, in place of the ragged scullery maid was an elegant princess. No longer an overgrown, crumbling haunted mansion but a stunning hotel with immaculate wallpaper, bathrooms perfectly tiled and towel-railed, manicured lawns, well-tended gardens and not a nettle in sight.

And again, unexpectedly but very happily, we were upgraded thanks to a booking error. Our one big room had originally been two but the owners had knocked out the dividing wall to make a spacious suite. The walls had been lovingly restored where possible and creatively renovated where not. It even had a tower bathroom almost identical to Cristallin's but firstly and most importantly, it was totally functional. And secondly, it had been tiled with images of elegant bathing ladies and whimsical mythical creatures. How they'd managed to get the tiles, vanity, shower and loo to fit in this oval tower was another miracle.

Not only was it a great way to end this part of our journey but it also gave us an unexpected opportunity to see how — with money, vision and talent — an ugly duckling of a château could be turned into a swan.

15. Merlin of High Hope Barn

Among all our many swaps and house sits, there were a few that really stood out, either for good or bad, but happily mostly for good. But the most wonderful of all was shared with one black cat, that enchanter and priest of nature, Merlin, Master of High Hope Barn. In fact, both Merlin and High Hope Barn were so wonderful that we double-dipped and went there twice, once in summer and a few months later in early autumn.

High Hope Barn was set high on a hill in the countryside of the Welsh Borders overlooking the Malvern Hills to the north, the Forest of Dean to the south, and the Black Mountains to the west. The closest city was Gloucester with nearby towns being Monmouth in England and Ross-on-Wye in Wales, while just a bit further on was our beloved book town, Hay-on-Wye.

As you might imagine, with a name like High Hope Barn, the first thing to strike us when driving up the steep rutted track of High Hope Hill was the panoramic view with nothing but fields, woods, hills and sky as far as the eye could see. Only the views from Las Grajeras in Spain came close to this stunner. Whether first thing on a misty morning, at high noon or at dusk with the sky ruby-red against the black hills, the view was breathtaking.

We were greeted by the charming, talented couple, Margaret and Jace, who'd lovingly restored the barn to create a home that oozed the shapes, colours and textures of Greece, India, Africa and the Far East but seamlessly melded with their very English settles, rustic dining tables and comfy sofas. Stone walls and flagstone floors can be dark and cold, but here, with its burgundy Turkish rugs, citrus and turquoise walls, coral-coloured candles and shelves of well-organised books, the barn was as warm and welcoming as we could wish. That is, except for the tall, thin, very spiky cactus camouflaged as a tall, thin post, that I accidentally clutched one day when putting on my boots.

Even on cold, windy days — and the wind could certainly howl around the barn perched so high on its hill — we enjoyed sitting in a kind of conservatory where the former barn doors had been replaced by huge glass windows. This light-filled area looked onto a colourful low-hedged garden just outside the window, the neighbouring house on the other side of the hilltop and to the meadows and hills beyond.

Margaret and Jace had obviously poured a lot of energy into creating a wonderful garden with sheltered nooks in the courtyard, artistic pebble groundcovers, a wildlife pond with eating-out platform, an orchard, meadow, vegetable gardens and flowerbeds. We felt so lucky knowing we'd have four glorious weeks watching the hollyhocks come into flower; gathering berries, peas and beans; visiting favourite spots such as Hay on Wye; and exploring new ones: the Forest of Dean, Monmouth and all those crumbling Welsh castles.

We soon fell into a very comfortable routine. First thing in the morning, Richard would go in search of Merlin. Unlike many other cats we'd looked after, he wasn't much of a people person and was happy either to head off bright and early through his cat flap into the garden or, as we soon discovered, have a bit of a lazy morning snooze in Jace's study.

One chilly morning soon after we'd arrived, Richard went looking for Merlin but he was nowhere to be found. Feeling a bit worried, we both started searching — upstairs, downstairs, in the courtyard and around the pond — to no avail. But one place we hadn't looked was *up*. Not upstairs but up near the ceiling. Backtracking through the downstairs rooms and into Jace's study, I looked up and noticed something odd. Above Jace's wraparound desk was a kind of mezzanine platform just below the ceiling, accessed by a set of wooden stairs. Memories of *Heidi*, one of my favourite childhood books, came to mind. When she'd gone to stay with her grandfather in his alpine cottage, Heidi delighted in sleeping in a little loft bed. Hmmm.... Could it be what I was thinking? I needed to climb up and investigate.

Now we'd seen many types of pet beds by this time, ranging from Smudge's sweet igloo and Red's huge plastic basket, to simple cushions and cardboard boxes but nothing prepared us for Merlin's sleeping quarters. Taking up the entire platform was a human-sized, neatly made loft bed. And there, slap in the middle of a very tasteful blanket, lay Merlin, curled in a soft black furry bundle, lazily turning his head to see who was disturbing his repose. Relief for us and breakfast for him.

After finding Merlin and organising breakfast it was garden-watering time. Usually in the UK, watering isn't much of an issue, simply because it rains so much. In recent years though, we've noticed that dry spells are much more common and this was the case for much of our early summer at High Hope Barn. Having extensive gardens is a treat but one that exacts a price: weeding and watering. Weeding wasn't an issue so early in the season but with such dry weather the vegetable gardens, flowerbeds and potted plants needed daily watering and because we were using watering cans rather than hoses, this was quite labour intensive.

We'd fill the cans from a couple of big tanks and when these were emptied, we had to pump water from the well that ran beneath the hill. This was all very interesting and fun in a way, except for the time that Richard couldn't stop water gushing out from the main water storage tank and we had visions of the entire water supply draining away before our eyes. In desperation he left me with a finger stuck in the tap spout like the Dutch boy in the dyke while he scoured the house in search of a wrench to turn it off. Merlin often accompanied us during our daily watering activities but on that day he was nowhere to be seen. His adventuring didn't extend to being soaked.

With so many places to explore on the Borders our days flew by while Merlin spent *his* days sunning himself in the drive, crouching in wait amongst the wildflowers around the pond, roaming in the meadow — and hunting. High Hope Barn was cat heaven with its abundant supply of field mice, rabbits and aquatic life, thanks to the pond.

As soon as our Merlin and garden duties were done, we'd make a beeline for a good coffee spot. One favourite was down the road at the Forest Bakehouse where a few rustic tables were squashed into the front of an airy shed where all the baking of bread, quiches and pies took place. Another favourite was Oscar's in Hay-on-Wye where we'd indulge in a slice of delicious apple cake made to an impossible-to-discover recipe.

Then, particularly if it was raining, we'd spend a few happy hours in Hay browsing among the book stores, or visiting one of the area's many National Trust properties, or doing a spot of shopping in the hilly little market town of Ross-on-Wye. For something a bit busier, there were two bigger towns and a city to choose from, each relatively close by and each with a totally different character.

Gloucester was the one nearest to us and although a bit shabby in parts, was perhaps the most dynamic, mainly because of its industrial heritage. Its position near the Severn estuary, along with the construction of canals and a railroad, had made it a trading hub in the 19th century but it had gradually declined, along with the shipping traffic. The regeneration of the docks area had been an imaginative effort to reinvent this part of the city, which unfortunately, had suffered from poor town planning and over-development in past years. With luck, this part of Gloucester with its old warehouses repurposed as trendy apartments and a new retail area with pedestrian-only plazas would bring money and new life into the heart of the city.

A bit further on was the Regency spa town of Cheltenham. Cheltenham was like Gloucester's well-dressed sister: elegant thanks to its Georgian architecture and with a sense of spaciousness thanks to its wide boulevards and location on a plain below the Cotswolds. Heritage was important too. Where Gloucester had docks and warehouses, Cheltenham had spas and a racetrack. Grit versus glamour!

Our town of choice though, was Monmouth on the Welsh side of the Borders. With its medieval gated bridge straddling the River Monnow, its bustling yet genteel high street with all our favourite shops — Marks & Spencer, Caffé Nero, Waitrose — and its intriguing alleys winding uphill from the river, this cheerful market town won our hearts.

On our return to High Hope Barn and if the weather was fine, we might take a walk around the meadow. And if we were very lucky and very blessed, Merlin would appear out of nowhere, his black coat studded with twigs and burs, and run along with us until side-tracked by some more interesting sight or sound — usually of the field mouse or baby rabbit variety.

In the evening he'd return for dinner and would sometimes join us in our favourite sunny snug or later in the sitting room as we watched TV. He was a joy to look after and so easy, with just a few occasional mouse-snack leftovers — neat little piles of organs — to remove from the mat at the bottom of his stairs.

One big surprise was discovering how popular the Arts and Crafts movement had been in this area. We knew that Chipping Campden had been an important centre but we didn't realise its reach had extended this far west. I was glad I'd mentioned this to Margaret since she too loved the style so had passed on tips about local places that we might never have discovered otherwise. Another benefit of house sitting.

Margaret had recommended visiting the nearby village of Kempley for two reasons: firstly, for its rarely held produce market and secondly, for its Arts and Crafts Church, St Edward's. Since I had no idea that such churches even existed, this was quite a find. The highlight was supposed to be the church and indeed it *was* lovely with its sculptures, tapestries and overall architectural design in the comfortingly symmetrical and spare style so typical of the movement. But the market was something else again.

It was a cold, blustery day — not great for driving but since it was our only chance to see the market, we made the effort. We were running late too because we'd been stuck behind a tractor on the winding single-lane country road that led into the village. We arrived just before it closed but luckily found a parking spot, though right on the edge of a dangerously deep ditch full of nettles, and made our way to the village hall. It seemed a bit weird when everyone we met — along the road, at the entrance gate and inside the hall itself — greeted us as if we were old friends.

It was actually a bit unnerving — a bit like one of those horror stories where the whole village is full of seemingly mild-mannered, genteel folk who are actually all in cahoots with the devil, luring unsuspecting newcomers who were destined to become part of their secret coven rituals. We certainly felt conspicuous. We hurriedly bought loads more strawberries than we'd ever eat, a loaf of crusty brown bread, a slice of peach tart and made our escape before we found ourselves in the crypt of St Edward's, surrounded by these chanting, smiling folk, now attired in their Arts and Crafts coven cloaks.

Oh dear. We'd obviously been horribly tainted by the evils of the Big Smoke of Sydney, London and Washington. It was clear that we really did need to get out into the country more, where people were simply just nice.

The British countryside is wonderful for walking and now, without any dogs to worry about, we were free to plan routes that took in churches and other buildings that would have been difficult with dogs in tow. Margaret and Jace had left us a useful book of walks, along with brochures and Ordnance Survey maps that Merlin found fascinating, wandering all over them whenever they were spread out on the coffee table. We'd often not see him for hours but as soon as we brought out a map, there he'd be, plonked right in the middle. Merlin was even more of an adventurer than we'd realised.

Summer walks have many advantages: long days, occasional good weather and with luck, no mud. But there is one disadvantage. Flies.

One walk we were keen to try was in the hills around Hay-on-Wye so we were relieved to set out under clear blue skies and looked forward to a mud-free walk. But what we hadn't counted on was doing battle with the millions of giant biting flies that descended upon us as we clumped through dried cow dung, clambered over broken stiles and tried to prevent our clothes from being snagged on barbed wire fences.

By the time we'd completed the circuit and once more saw Hay spread out in the valley below, we were horribly bitten, footsore and parched. But to our immense relief, we soon found a tavern, the Beer Revolution, with rough-hewn wooden tables, retro '60s vinyl chairs, beer and cider. It wasn't a walk we'd try again, especially in summer, but if it hadn't been for its trials and tribulations, we would never have staggered into that eccentric tavern which immediately joined our favourites' list.

The Forest of Dean sculpture trail was a much more dependable bet. With well-marked paths, no cattle to attract giant biting flies or horses to churn up the dirt paths, we could walk and chat at the same time or simply enjoy the forest — and the sculptures. And since Margaret had told us how her uncle had helped set up the sculpture trail when he worked for the Forestry Commission, there was an added incentive to visit.

Forests are wonderful in themselves but here the whole woodsy experience had been enhanced by the many sculptures throughout that helped marry the natural beauty of today's forest with its grittier industrial past. Many had been created using natural materials from the forest such as stone or wood, but many were man-made, like the iron railroad tracks that had been brought in during the coal mining days. Others were hidden away so coming across them brought an added element of delight, while others made a statement, standing proudly on open ground.

Coal mining had been one of the Forest's main industries throughout the 19th century and well into the 20th. It was hard to imagine this now-peaceful spot as a hive of activity with railroads running throughout, carrying their loads of coal. We wondered too, what life must have been like for all those miners. The job itself must have been physically awful especially in winter, leaving home on those dark mornings to head into the even more oppressive darkness of the pit, only to emerge in the afternoon gloom. We take our central heating, washing machines and dryers for granted so it was sobering to imagine what it must have been like for those wives and mothers battling to wash bodies, clothes and boots, with clothes lines stretched between the walls of their workers' cottages or on racks in the kitchen, the air heavy with black coal dust.

It was from the harshness of such lives, along with the famed miners' camaraderie, that trade unions emerged as a way of fighting against financial exploitation and dangerous working conditions. Such reminders of how harsh life used to be are useful antidotes to complacency. So very gratefully we returned from our thought-provoking walk through time to the warm, dry and coal-dust-free snug at High Hope Barn.

Our autumn sit at High Hope Barn was a delight, what with the magical vanishing Merlin, ripening corn, late berries from the garden and evenings spent watching the sun sink in reddening skies below the dark hills.

Cows featured quite a bit during our time on the Borders, as did churches and castles. During our autumn stint at High Hope Barn, we made these our focus — not so much the cows, which were simply unavoidable — but churches and castles. Now with cooler but generally fine weather we could do some of the walks we'd not managed to do in summer.

The most interesting and varied of the church walks followed a circular route starting at the 13th century St John's Church in King's Caple. This was the sort of church we'd come to expect in most English villages. It was old, of medium size and very traditional inside and out. Near the entrance alongside some information leaflets, parishioners had generously placed baskets of apples and jugs of water for passing visitors to enjoy. It was the quintessential English village church — simple and with a heart.

There was, however, one discordant element. Being autumn, the churchgoers had set up a harvest festival display. We'd seen these in other churches over the years, with varying degrees of creativity on display along with the produce. Here in this small village church with its presumably small congregation, the display with its few fruits and vegetables was a little meagre and not exactly a work of art. But love and care had obviously been put into its creation and anyhow, it didn't matter how beautiful it was. This was a tribute to the harvest, a little reminder of how grateful we should be for the fruits of the land and those who work on it. So I was shocked when I saw that some small-minded and distinctly *un*generous person had commented in the visitors' book that this was the worst harvest display they'd ever seen.

I felt so badly for the little congregation that I added my own comment thanking them for their kindness and generosity, hoping they'd read mine first and perhaps miss the nasty one above. Was this perhaps a symptom of our current Twitter age? No longer did we sing of careless whispers but instead, tapped out careless insults.

From King's Caple, we headed through someone's orchard, crossed an unusual pedestrian suspension bridge to the other side of the River Wye, and made our way through a meadow to a very different church, St Tysilio's at Sellack. This was so old, tiny and unexpectedly odd that it was actually more memorable than our visits to any of the grand cathedrals.

As we wandered around the little grassy churchyard trying to find a way in, a scruffy-looking man appeared, hot and dusty from ground work which, we assumed, was nothing more than mowing and weeding. He cheerfully put aside his tools and apologised for his unkempt state. It turned out he wasn't a workman per se but a churchwarden and he'd been busy reinterring 400-year-old human remains, possibly plague victims, which had been discovered during recent renovation work. It isn't every day you stumble across a smiling, chatty gentleman taking a break from reburying ancient bones.

Taking us inside he gave us a brief but fascinating history of the church and its patron saint, the Celtic St Tysilio, who sounded like a 7th century peacenik and quite a rebel when it came to withstanding family pressure to toe the line. Then pointing to some plain glass windows over the altar, our warden-guide explained that they had been damaged by a bunch of vandals. And then, after a brief dramatic pause, he added — Cromwell and his gang!

I was starting to really enjoy this church. I told him that if I lived round this neck of the woods, I'd like to join in, what with burying plague victims, Cromwell's brief but nasty visit, and St Tysilio's go-it-alone stance. But there was one sticking point — I was a non-believer.

No problem, he assured me. I wouldn't be the only one. In fact I'd probably enjoy their monthly discussion group where all kinds of issues pertaining to faith, or lack thereof, were openly explored.

I meant it though. The warden was inspirational: warm, friendly, funny and with no agenda apart from sharing his time, his love of the church and showing kindness.

After leaving St Tysilio's, we got lost. Our book of walks let us down once again as we found ourselves at the end of a muddy path leading to a field and old farmhouse rather than the road we'd been expecting. While we stood there bewildered and scrutinising our map, a lady emerged from the farmhouse and came to our rescue. Not only was she helpful but she was also unexpectedly diverting as she related how she'd moved from the flat Canadian prairies to try this very different rural life in the rolling hills of the Welsh Borders. A fellow traveller, in every sense of the word.

We skirted the bottom of her farmhouse, cut through another field and eventually reached the last church of our walk, St Catherine's at Hoarwithy, which was the complete opposite of simple St Tysilio's. A relatively recent build from the mid-19th century, it was beautiful but in a very strange way. You just don't expect to see an Italian hilltop church with arcades, colourful tiled floors and a light-filled, pink marble interior deep in the English countryside. All three churches were so different that I would hate to have missed any one of them — though I still have a very soft spot for St Tysilio's.

And so to castles and cows. The Borders are famed for the many ruined medieval castles built as a defence against Welsh rebels so we planned many of our walks around these sites. When friends, Avis and Peter, arrived for a short visit and since they were keen walkers, we wanted to take them somewhere special. So after consulting Margaret and Jace's book of walks, we chose one that would take us from the Skenrith Castle ruins, along a stream, up a hill to Garway Church, over more fields and back to Skenrith. Ideal. An easy walk with a nice variety of castle, river, church and fields.

So off we set on a cool but clear day and had a quick look around the crumbling ruins of Skenrith before heading off on our ramble along the tumbling River Monnow. The trees were just turning pale gold and there was not a person to be seen. Bliss!

Garway Church was also unusual, boasting a pagan green man carving as well as a Knights Templar sword. It was always a bonus finding something unexpectedly eccentric. After passing a few scattered cottages, Avis stopped at a farmyard gate to buy some eggs from a little stall with an honesty box. And then the heavens opened.

Gales, pouring rain, umbrellas blown inside out — and we still had all those fields to get through before making it back to the car. We picked our way through a brambly hedge and across a field, the cowpats now soggy from the rain, and to make things worse, a herd of around twenty cows was advancing towards us. Remembering advice about what to do when encountering animals in the wild, we stumbled as fast as we could over grassy knolls and cowpats, avoiding any eye contact while still furtively checking where they were — unfortunately, still determinedly heading our way.

Safety was in sight when we finally spotted a stile at the bottom of the field. Clutching umbrellas, eggs and bags we made one final dash, arriving at the stile at the same time as the cows. But still we had to pick our way through the huge mud and cowpat bog at the stile's base, clamber over it while trying to avoid the bird droppings, now wet and sticky from rain, and cross the thankfully cow-free neighbouring field.

At least from there on it was downhill, the rain eased off and we gratefully reached our car, now sitting in a giant mud puddle beside the castle ruins. That evening, dinner at the aptly named Moody Cow pub seemed in order.

Sadly the next day was our last at High Hope Barn and very nearly Merlin's, when we discovered him camouflaged amongst our bags in the back seat just as we were getting ready to leave. We'd had two wonderful visits, first in early summer and later in autumn, and were beginning to feel very much at home among the Borders.

So we bade a fond farewell to this gentle, beautiful place and all its animals — even the cows — and left Merlin to his hunting and magical vanishing acts.

16. Perfect Homes, Endearing Pets

Pet and house sitting is always a bit of a gamble with a few elements in play that, if not to your satisfaction, can spoil the adventure. Luckily this was a rare occurrence, especially once we gained some experience and began learning the possible pitfalls and becoming alert to the danger signals.

For us there were two key elements: the pets and the homes. If we got these two things right we always had an enjoyable time. And when the owners were welcoming and generous in spirit, we'd hit the jackpot.

We certainly hit the jackpot at High Hope Barn. The home was not just comfortable and spacious but was also a sensory delight, decorated with exotic flair in books, artworks and colourful crockery. And it was just as lovely outside with a walled courtyard, vegetable gardens and breathtaking views. Merlin the black cat had almost totemic power, representing adventure, independence and endless curiosity but was also just fun to hang out with — when he graced us with his presence. And to top it off, Jace and Margaret were a warm-hearted couple who welcomed us with tasty meals, copious glasses of wine, fascinating tales and loads of laughter.

In Spain the high point was the imaginatively renovated Las Grajeras. The farmhouse was modern, easy to manage and as with High Hope Barn, just as lovely outside as in, with its terraced gardens and panoramic views over endless olive groves. Rossi the black dog was our constant companion and one of those endearing pets we could happily have taken home with us. And again, owners Sylvia and David were such fun to be with, getting us straight into the Spanish vibe by introducing us to some tapas bars that we'd never have discovered on our own.

But there were a few other standout sits that we felt very lucky to have found, jackpots every one.

For Hamptons-style elegance and misty-eyed pet memories, the prize goes to a wintry long weekend sit at the Lodge near Haslemere on England's South Downs. We'd been given precise instructions that would take us down a busy A road; continue along a series of ever narrower, less frequented roads; and then down a private unpaved lane until we came to a lamp post beside a pair of wooden gates. Naturally, in the darkening gloom of a February evening, the final stretch wasn't easy. However, we eventually made it to this last, very dark and winding lane, with huge trees and bushes looming on either side, to find the lamp post, its pale light beckoning through the evening mist, beside some wooden gates — just as promised.

It was a bit like something out of *The Lion, the Witch and the Wardrobe* as we drove through the gates and entered another world, though since it was by then pitch dark, we didn't appreciate its full magnificence until morning. Owners, Rita and Keith, greeted us with a greatly appreciated gin and tonic, followed by butternut squash risotto cooked on their massive Aga cooker, which, as I was now well aware, would provide me with a challenge or two. But that evening Rita, the expert, produced a perfect risotto, tricky enough to get right on a regular cooker, especially when chatting and trying to impart vital pet-sitting information.

Seated on stools around the central island of their expansive open-plan kitchen we gazed upon the rest of the family, dining and sitting rooms. Our entire cottage in Chipping Campden would easily have fitted into just this space alone. Later we retired to our reassuringly pretty bedroom that overlooked the front garden, now pitch black, and had a very good night's sleep.

Rita and Keith headed off to Heathrow in the wee hours of the morning but by the time we awoke much later at sunrise, the full extent of their property was revealed. From our bedroom window we surveyed a world of gravel drives, sweeping lawns, sunken ponds and a slightly overgrown mossy tennis court. Even the garden shed and garage were picturesque with matching potted miniature trees on either side of every door.

The biggest surprise though was to discover that the huge open-plan room where we'd had dinner the previous evening made up only a fraction of the ground floor. We were eating breakfast at the kitchen island, gazing out at this vast garden, when, wanting a closer look from the French doors that opened onto the terrace, we noticed a little window in a side wall. Peeking through we saw yet one more world, and yet another series of expansive rooms. Rita and Keith had told us that they'd done an extensive renovation but we had no idea it had been that extensive.

So in full explorer mode we headed back up the few steps to the kitchen and into the hallway. On one side we discovered a large, comfortable sitting room with open fireplace and more French doors opening onto another terrace and the gardens beyond. Beside the fireplace yet more doors took us to the room we'd just seen from the family room. Perhaps this room was the most intriguing of all, being a music room-cum-library with every paperback I'd either read or wanted to read, as well as all our favourite CDs — Pink Floyd, Genesis, Electric Light Orchestra — plus a glossy black, fully operational grand piano. Heading back through the sitting room and across the hallway, we found a cheery little snug with two sofas and a TV. From one extreme to the other.

As soon as I'd walked through the front door the evening before, it was clear that Rita was a lover of symmetry, as am I, so I took great interest in how she'd perfectly balanced every shelf, window ledge and mantelpiece. Her palette was neutral, elegant and calming: pale greys in the sitting rooms, soft limes and yellows in the snug, and her soft furnishings featured the natural textures of crumpled linen and embossed cottons.

So two big ticks to the Manor. One — delightful owners and two — a home that wasn't just magazine-cover gorgeous but also a place of comfort, good cheer and serenity. This was a home not so much aiming to impress but rather to enhance the well-being of anyone who was lucky enough to spend time there. And then there was tick number three — the pets.

Now since this chapter focuses on particularly *endearing* pets, I must make the point that out of the two pets residing at the Lodge, Tiggie the cat and Mabel the dog, Tiggie was not so much endearing as forgettable. In fact, Rita had told me she'd forgotten him herself a few times so I don't feel too bad saying this. He was totally easy-care and although he had an entire house to roam in, he mostly hunkered down inside the snug's TV cabinet. We only discovered this when on our first morning we tried searching for him throughout all those many downstairs rooms and the two floors above, only to get the shock of our lives when, having given up, we went to turn on the TV. And there he was, snug as a bug in his snug, happily curled up on the top shelf of the TV cabinet.

But as for Mabel — she was an adorable ten-year-old pointer with (naturally) symmetrically patterned black and white stripes down her back and legs. She stayed glued to us throughout our stay but was so well trained that whenever we were cooking or eating she kept to her pale-hued beds and cushions, all suitably positioned in every room — usually in front of a fireplace. When not reclining on one of these, she'd try to stand directly under someone's hand, exactly within stroking reach.

We took her on walks during the day but as the gardens were so extensive, we only needed to walk her around the periphery a few times a day so there were no muddy paths, churned-up bridleways or cows to cope with. Although she followed us everywhere while we were in the house, she never attempted to climb onto the furniture and was happy to settle into her kitchen basket at night.

In our short time at the Lodge we took the opportunity to do a bit of entertaining since Haslemere was within reasonable driving distance of friends and family. Cooking on the Aga was again a challenge but with moral support and a little bit of help from our friends, together with one relatively simple menu, we managed.

Just as a reminder, with Aga cookers there are basically two settings for the hobs — hot and very hot — and two for the ovens — hot and warmish. Spaghetti bolognaise turned out to be a wise choice as nothing much can go wrong with that. But even then I found myself shuffling the sauce between the hot and very hot hobs while I cooked the pasta, eventually realizing that I could keep the sauce warm in the warmish oven while I kept my eye on the pasta on the hot hob. The only problem with this plan was that I'd made an apple crumble for dessert, which was browning in the hot oven but it too needed to be shifted to the warmish one to avoid being burned. There just weren't enough warm versus hot hobs. I repeated this menu a couple of times so after the successful spaghetti but undercooked crumble the first time round, I'd cracked it by the second, finally achieving spaghetti and crumble perfection.

One day we took a day off from entertaining on the Aga and tried out a local pub, the Duke of Cumberland, which had wonderful views over the South Downs. We imagined how lovely it would be in summer, sitting at one of the wooden tables in the terraced gardens or in one of the many nooks and crannies hidden amongst its hillocky setting. But even though it was winter and so very busy inside, it was still a delight with welcoming open fires, flagstone floors, dogs everywhere and tasty food. It's always a bonus when house sitting if there's a well-patronized, atmospheric pub nearby.

On our last day Mabel was very poorly, not interested in walking and would eat nothing at all. We knew she must have been really ill when she left our company and took to her bed in the snug. As it was our last afternoon we became quite worried when we checked on her before leaving and found her lying in her basket, groaning a little in her sleep. I'd already contacted Rita who'd reassured us, saying Mabel's colitis occasionally flared up but still, we did feel very badly for her. Tiggie, though, was still in his snug TV bed and totally oblivious to poor Mabel's sore tummy.

Calm, comfortable elegance, an easy cat and a dear dog — luck had been with us at the Lodge.

Next was another completely renovated home, the Manor in Driffield, a village on the other side of England just outside the ancient Roman town of Cirencester.

As this was a summer pet sit, we arrived in full daylight, which made navigation easy, as did the route along easy-to-follow roads rather than the off-piste lanes of Haslemere. We drove down a gravelled tree-lined drive with expansive lawns and colourful herbaceous borders, past a formal garden and fountain sheltered by hornbeam hedges to finally arrive at the honey-gold Cotswold stone house. As with so many sits, we were warmly greeted by the owners and treated to a tasty home-cooked meal, wine and conversation — always a great way to start a pet sit.

Their home was equally lovely in the crisp, breezy Hamptons style that I adore. But I was surprised by the unexpectedly dramatic décor of our huge bedroom with its navy walls, bright white woodwork and a fantastically free-form silver and navy bedhead. Then there was the den — a veritable man cave with plush indigo carpet, crimson walls, white floor-to-ceiling bookshelves and zebra-print armchairs. Where the Lodge excelled in subtle, symmetrical harmony, the Manor amazed with wow-factor daring.

Archie, our only responsibility (another plus) was a miniature Schnauzer with attitude. Owners Terri and Richard had told us that he wasn't allowed on the carpets, the furniture or upstairs. Just like the adorable Jet in Cornwall, he was only a few months old and also like Jet, he really did obey these house rules. Well, most of the time.

He loved running off with balls, soft toys and unfortunately, shoes and socks. We tried remembering to leave our shoes high up on the stairs out of sight but sometimes he managed to catch a glimpse and if we weren't around, the temptation was too much. We'd only realize he'd made off with one of our shoes or socks when he appeared, in ready-to-play mode, with the stolen item hanging from his jaw. Then, just as we made a grab for it, he'd dart off, gleefully running round the garden having a whale of a time. This game was fine if we were playing with a ball or one of his stuffed toys, Foxy or Rudolf, but it was very frustrating when trying to retrieve a vital shoe just as we were heading out the door.

It was fascinating to see how he worked around the no-going-on-carpet rule. We'd spend the evenings in the snug, an elegant yet comfortable room with two small sofas and against the furthest wall, one of Archie's dog beds. The room was carpeted but the entrance hall just outside had timber floors so Archie was perfectly comfortable sitting out there — both physically and emotionally. We'd be on the sofas watching TV and he'd be lying outside looking in until suddenly, he'd dart across the carpet and leap into his basket. I always offered to carry him in each evening but for some strange reason known only to him, he preferred to sit in the hall and bide his time till he was ready to do his mad carpet dash. Maybe it was one of his games — waiting till our attention was distracted and seeing if he could leap into his basket before we noticed.

It was even more fascinating watching how Archie managed to join us in the den. The den had two entrances: one was from the timber-floored hallway and the other was from the outside terrace. He'd happily follow us down the hall to the den door but as soon as we stepped onto the carpet, he'd stop, pause for a moment and then turn around to race back down the hall, through the kitchen and across the terrace to the outside door. Very canny because that part of the den had timber flooring. There was no way he'd disobey that no-carpet rule.

His sleeping arrangements worked seamlessly too. In the round conservatory-style foyer was his toy box against one wall and his crate with comfy bed on the other. Here he'd happily settle each evening with his ration of treats and toy of the day and there he'd stay, warm and snug, until we came to let him out in the morning.

With so many delightful pubs around we didn't need to cook for the few friends who came to visit but a quick aperitif while watching Archie's playful antics was *de rigueur*. Our Cheltenham friend Pamela participated more directly when Archie made off with one of her shoes and she unwisely attempted to try and catch him. This, we'd learnt from hard experience, just added fuel to his fire. There was nothing he loved more than playing this chasing game. Once we'd chased him round the garden beds, lawn, formal garden and little wood trying to retrieve a pigeon trailing from his jaw. By the time he'd tired of the game, the poor bird was hanging by a thread of sinew in a mangled mess. Still, we didn't try to stop Pamela. How often do you see an octogenarian, dressed to the nines, chasing a mischievous little dog joyfully making off with her shoe?

We did try taking Archie to one of the nicest pubs in the area, the dog- and horse-friendly Bell at Sapperton. Being a lovely sunny day we sat outside in the garden but as he was showing a bit too much interest in the other dogs, we thought it best to tie him to a table leg. That was when we discovered just how strong a miniature Schnauzer could be. These outside tables were big, hefty wooden things yet within minutes of settling him there at our feet, Archie was off and away after a neighbouring dog, nearly taking our table with him. Luckily he gave a wide berth to the horses tethered to the railing.

An unanticipated pleasure we gained from travelling in this mode was seeing rural life up close. Driffield was surrounded by fields and a meandering stream so on our walks with Archie we enjoyed watching the harvesting of the late summer crops and chatting to farm workers. At the back of one farmhouse there was some shed construction going on with music blaring from a radio that the workmen had set up outside, a common practice anywhere. But this was the first time we'd ever encountered builders listening to Classic FM while they worked.

A high-toned village indeed, with its perfect homes, perfect gardens and almost perfectly trained pets. Archie was one very lucky dog.

For countryside comfort, peaceful surroundings and pet appeal, a converted barn in West Sussex also ticked all the boxes. We'd met owners, Phil and Tony, a few weeks earlier when they'd invited us to a magnificent lunch so we could meet and discuss general arrangements. What wasn't to like, with a pre-lunch Pimm's on the terrace overlooking the rose garden with wooded hills beyond, followed by salmon, new potatoes and a homemade pavlova piled high with cream and berries? And most impressive of all, Phil managed all this on her Aga. Now the bar was set far higher. I really needed to expand my spaghetti and fruit crumble repertoire.

So when we arrived for our week in early autumn, we knew exactly what we could look forward to: a beautifully converted barn on a quiet valley road with guest suite at one end, kitchen and living areas in the middle, and sunny conservatory at the far end. The surrounding garden, with its apple orchard and hedges separating the barn from adjoining fields, could be seen from every window. It truly was a home of tranquillity and beauty. Not magazine-cover gorgeous as with the Lodge or drop-dead dramatic as with the Manor, but an easy-care mélange of country comfort living areas, crisp Scandinavian bedrooms and English country garden — with a traditional hunting dog to complete the picture.

Alfie was a liver and white English Springer Spaniel and true to his breed, he adored birds — hunting them that is. On our first rapid dash by car to check out nearby dog-walking sites, Phil had made a point of dismissing some trails because of 'Pheasant!' We didn't quite understand the significance of this until we took Alfie out on our first morning walk. We managed to get him across the road and over a stile into the field opposite easily enough but once he heard a rustling in the hedge, he was off. Trying to call him back once he'd spotted a pheasant was impossible. No amount of coaxing with treats or angry shouts would keep him from his main goal in life — catching a pheasant. And if it wasn't a pheasant, it was catching a ball, and if not a ball, a windfall apple would do just fine.

We knew Alfie was a rescue dog, one of many owned by neighbours who, realizing they had one dog too many, managed to find him a good home with Phil and Tony. After the first couple of days we started to see why his original owners might have chosen him as their cull dog because, adorable as he was, he could be a handful. He was so nice to stroke with his silky brown and white fur and so cheerful to have around, sitting in his kitchen basket with his favourite ball while I attempted to conquer the Aga. We grew uneasy though if we were outside and he suddenly vanished into one of the hedges. Then we knew trouble was brewing because that's where he made most of his successful pheasant conquests.

In comparison to Merlin's little field mice or Archie's slightly larger pigeons, Alfie's pheasant victims were enormous. He delighted in catching them, proudly displaying what he'd caught — none of this running off in a chasing game as with Archie — but simple animal pleasure in chomping and chewing, with his prey's wings and legs shamelessly splayed. After a couple of days, all that remained would be a pile of entrails and the next day, just a few feathers. During our one-week stay, he managed to polish off at least three of these unlucky birds.

As for the Aga, I'm afraid that rather than improving on my cooking skills, the opposite occurred. Thinking it was best to start from the known and gradually progress to newer challenges, my first attempt was to bake an apple crumble, something relatively easy. But what with chatting, having fun with Alfie and juggling between the warmish, hot and very hot ovens, we unfortunately had semi-burnt offerings that day. The next day's baked apples were a bit of an improvement but by then I'd accepted the inevitable. Sadly I wouldn't have enough time to perfect my Aga-cooking skills. Fortunately, though, we remembered that Phil had told us about a farm shop not far away that did wonderful gourmet pre-cooked meals. So for the rest of our stay I swallowed my pride and we ate very well indeed from its selection of lamb tagine, coq au vin and lasagne — all perfectly cooked and stress free.

Pheasant feathers and entrails aside, we were sad to leave this mellow barn with its lush green lawns, nestled among golden fields and rolling hills. It was perfectly quiet at night with clear, starry skies but also just a short drive from the cathedral city of Chichester — the best of both worlds. One lolloping, silky smooth, loving dog with a talent for pheasant hunting enhanced the experience, as we'd only owned city dogs ourselves. Trying out life with gun dogs was new and fun but not for the queasy.

17. Space Invaders

Fortunately, our misses and close shaves were few and far between. We've heard a few horror stories about arriving in homes with unmade beds, piled-up washing, more animals than expected and battered sofas covered with papers, toys and half-eaten dog biscuits. We've also heard of events unforeseen by the owners such as appliances breaking down, flooding from broken pipes and the sudden death of a pet. So all in all, we've counted ourselves very lucky. However, there will inevitably be the occasional disappointment and of course, the more sits you do, the greater the chance of a dud.

When I analyse which sits I'd consider 'misses' and 'close shaves', one common element stands out — space. By this I mean both physical space, such as whether you'd have enough room to unpack or would have to live out of a suitcase and personal space, which is more about privacy and being able to have time out.

One particular bugbear, particularly with lengthier sits or exchanges, is arriving with a few bags of supplies only to discover the fridge and pantry already jam-packed and the cabinets so crammed with pots and pans that there'd be no way you'd even attempt to pull anything out, let alone want to try fitting it back again.

We arrived at one house swap in a spectacular but isolated mountain area with instructions to empty the fridge/freezer and leave the doors open on our departure in case of freezing weather. This was a perfectly sensible request and we'd organised our supplies so we'd have hardly anything to dispose of when we left. The only trouble was that both fridge and freezer were already full when we arrived so we had to empty dozens of bottles and jars and dispose of bags of frozen food that we'd never be able to use. Since we try to never waste food ourselves, it was an annoying and time-consuming exercise. But never fear — you'll find some coping strategies and prevention advice in chapter 20.

As for human space invaders, our first dog sit at the stables was fine until the extended family descended on us and took over the house, apart from our bedroom, leaving us as the space invaders. It was their family home after all. The bigger problem was that we became the 'hired help', adding an unwelcome layer of resentment to an already difficult situation. Originally we had two dogs to look after at night and three during the day but with four it became an imposition. In that case though, there was nothing that we could have done to avoid it and it was certainly not the owners' fault. But after that experience, we were much more vigilant in gathering as much information as we could when arranging a sit.

Even so, we had a couple of close shaves and one definite miss but there was still a silver lining. I've already told the story of the close shave in Cornwall with the menagerie in the mill house over Christmas. It wasn't so bad in the living room or kitchen but sharing the bedroom with a giant-sized cat jungle gym, a tank of amphibians and scores of stuffed toys was a definite turn-off. Add to that the variety and sheer number of animals — rabbits, cats, dogs, newts, toads, fish and possibly more as in my shocked state I could easily have missed some — we knew our space would definitely be limited. We definitely had a lucky escape there.

❦

Another was in Berkshire, close to where we had lived a few years earlier. This appealed because we thought we'd be able to entertain friends who still lived in the area and so repay them for all their hospitality over the last few months. The house seemed lovely on the website: a beautifully renovated character cottage with a leafy garden and on a quiet lane. We'd be looking after two rescue dogs, which we were perfectly happy about but the owners did stress that an aged relative would be living downstairs. They assured us that she wouldn't impose but if we could just check on her now and then, they'd be grateful. All seemed absolutely fine. We'd happily pop into her granny flat for a friendly chat, pick up anything she needed when we went shopping and also provide her with a bit of security.

Fortunately though, we arranged to visit well ahead of their planned departure and were very glad we did. The house was a beautifully renovated Victorian cottage set in a private, leafy garden and the owners were delightful. The dogs were friendly and seemed to be problem free, which isn't always the case with rescue dogs. We've generally found them to be endearing, especially if they've clearly suffered in their former lives, but they aren't always so well trained, for obvious reasons. One memorable exception was Scruff, one of the two dogs we'd looked after in Treignac. Although rescued from the streets of Cardiff, he was actually very well trained despite his years as a vagabond but he was also very crafty and nimble when it came to breaking and entering.

However, the problem here again was space. As we were shown around the house, it became heart-sinkingly clear that there was no granny flat for the aged relative and that 'downstairs' meant every room on the ground floor apart from the eat-in kitchen. The lovely sitting and dining rooms that opened onto the terrace and garden had been repurposed as a separate flat, which was lovely for her but it didn't take much imagination to see what our living arrangements would be like.

The kitchen-diner had a table and chairs squashed into the kitchen part and in the diner half where the table should have been were two small sofas, with one large dog on each. I visualised coming back from woodland walks with two muddy dogs, washing them off in the utility room beside the kitchen and spending the day with them in these cramped quarters — and it wasn't a pretty picture. Any thoughts of genteel Sunday lunches with friends when squashed between the kitchen cabinets and then fighting for space with these two friendly but very determined sofa-hogging dogs faded very rapidly indeed. It was as clear as day that this was a sit we'd have to back away from. It was definitely *not* a win/win situation but still, we were relieved that we were only at the beginning of our discussions, allowing the owners plenty of time to regroup.

So now for the sit that we couldn't back away from and which, unfortunately, was to be the lengthiest of them all.

I can't say I didn't do my vetting — as much as that's possible from thousands of miles away. We'd been back in Sydney for a few months after returning from our mega-trip based in Chipping Campden and were starting to organise some shorter sits for the following year. One listing seemed perfect. It was near Oxford — a perfect location — was for a nice long chunk of time — six weeks — and it would be in summer.

We had quite a few email exchanges and a couple of very pleasant Skype conversations with Christina, the lady of the house, while her not-so-tech-savvy husband Alan sat reading behind her on the living room sofa. From what we could see of the sitting room, it looked like a comfortable, traditionally furnished room with a cream leather lounge suite and some bookshelves. The two dogs, pug Bambi and Labrador Lulu, seemed well behaved. We checked the property out on Google Earth and all seemed fine. It was a terrace house in the countryside with fields and hills directly behind, a two-lane road to the front and beyond that was the main part of the village, which looked delightful.

We were to be away for four months: all of summer into early autumn. This summer sit would form the core of our trip, bookended on either side by a few weeks with Merlin at High Hope Barn.

We'd left High Hope Barn, after removing the ever-adventurous Merlin from the back seat where his black fur was nicely camouflaged against our luggage, and headed off in good spirits for this long summer sit in Oxfordshire. We felt a little sad as we prised Merlin from our suitcases and drove down the steep hill and away from High Hope Barn with its just-opening hollyhocks but we knew we'd be back in autumn, for which we were truly grateful.

A couple of hours later as we drove through our new Oxfordshire village, trying to read house numbers without being rammed from behind by a disturbingly steady stream of traffic, we felt the first stirrings of doubt. The pretty little terrace we'd *kind* of seen on Google Earth was a lot shabbier and a lot closer to the road than we'd imagined. Still, we thought, things would improve once we were inside.

After driving round the block a few times we finally found the back entrance in a lane behind the terraces' back gardens and located the correct gate, ominously broken with half the palings either jaggedly splintered or simply missing. Still, we told ourselves, a gate is just a gate. Our gate back home wasn't in such great shape either — not that bad, but still — we were just being overly sensitive and picky after leaving the glories of High Hope Barn. So in through the gate we went, across the lawn with its bedraggled garden beds to the back door where we were greeted by Christina, Alan and the two dogs.

After a very warm welcome, supper and a couple of bottles of wine in the farmhouse kitchen, things were starting to look up. We still hadn't gone further than the kitchen and living room but spending such an enjoyable evening in such good company cheered us up immensely. So what if the back gate was falling apart, the garden was a mess and the house exterior was in sore need of some attention. The owners were friendly, the dogs seemed well behaved, and the ambiance, that night at least, was pleasant enough.

I began growing a little edgy as midnight approached and we were still chatting around the kitchen table. We hadn't been shown our room yet and our bags were still sitting in the living room so I was relieved when finally Christina suggested that it might be time to call it a night and get us settled in. And that's when my earlier forebodings were justified.

The living room had lots of bookshelves. There was nothing particularly remarkable about that and in fact, it was quite pleasing. However, as we went up the stairs, across the landing and into our room, it was clear that every inch of wall space and even the stairs themselves had been invaded by books — books they must have owned since childhood and many possibly inherited from their parents as well. Every book they'd ever read must have been in that house. Some were piled so high and in such inaccessible places that even if anyone *wanted* to pull one out from the bottom of a twenty-book-high pile, it would be almost impossible. In our room too, the bed was pushed up against an entire wall of floor-to-ceiling bookshelves. The mind boggled wondering how anyone would go about retrieving a book from the top shelves or even trickier, from beneath the bed, which would certainly require a torch and a fair bit of dusty crawling.

The next shock was seeing the window coverings, or rather lack of window coverings. A few weeks earlier we'd watched the TV series *Midnight Sun*, set in the far north of Sweden at the height of summer and whose main character was nearly driven to distraction by the sun beaming into her bedroom window throughout most of the night. Christina herself actually pointed out this lack of window coverings, simply saying that there were no blinds or curtains but it wouldn't be a problem. Not one to make a fuss, I hesitated briefly. But seven weeks of sleeping in a room where I'd be awake at sunrise, around 4 a.m. in summer, was absolutely going to be a problem. Christina took this in good spirits, cheerily remarking that it wouldn't matter anyway because the noise from the road would probably wake us even earlier than the sun. Misgivings, misgivings, misgivings!

Now one unusual aspect of this sit was that although we'd agreed to stay for seven weeks, the owners had planned three distinct holidays, returning home for a few days after each one. This meant we'd all be living in the house together during those times or, as Christina suggested, we might like to take the opportunity to take a little holiday ourselves. At that stage we hadn't made any plans to go anywhere else, thinking we'd play it be ear.

And play it by ear we certainly did. Our first night did not bode well. As our hosts left us to settle in for the night and headed downstairs, through the living areas and up the other side to their quarters, we soon discovered that their quarters were actually in the room directly adjoining ours, separated by a thin door with a huge gap underneath. Since we could hear them chatting quite clearly, we were reduced to whispering. Staying there during their return visits would be tricky enough when sharing living quarters but sharing conversations at night as well wasn't the least bit appealing.

The road outside was the main route through the village and though not super busy, it did carry a fair amount of traffic. But it wasn't just the noise that was disturbing; it was also the headlights that flashed in through the uncovered windows as cars drove past. With this happening at frequent intervals in the wee hours and knowing that the sun would soon rise, it was hardly surprising that I barely slept a wink. One night of broken sleep was bearable but we had seven weeks ahead of us. Action was needed. Bailing wasn't an option — they were nice people and anyway, we'd made a commitment that was impossible at that stage to break.

So Richard, being a very handy man, took off to a hardware store first thing in the morning and returned with a couple of sheets of heavy black card from which he created makeshift window shutters. For the rest of our stay these went up every night while earplugs went in. Problem solved. However, we did decide that on the occasions when Christina and Alan returned, we'd make ourselves scarce and head off, Merlin-like, for a weekend's rest and recreation.

Now to the dogs. Leila was an old, almost toothless, virtually deaf and patient golden Labrador. She was a joy to be with apart from three things. Firstly, we had to watch her carefully on walks when off leash or anywhere near cars; secondly, she was an excellent jumper and could nab food within jumping reach on any surface; and thirdly, she sat on all the furniture, a behaviour we were increasingly growing to dislike. Bambi though was our main concern. She was a pug, a breed we'd not dealt with before, so it was a shock to see just how unhealthy this breed could be and also to discover that it was the breeders, and indirectly the purchasers, who had created these very problems.

It didn't take long to notice that Bambi was very different from all the other dogs we'd cared for. On our first walk up the track to the top of the hill behind the house, she came willingly enough. Leila ran off, oblivious to our calls but safe on the track, while poor Bambi held up the rear, snuffling and snorting, collapsing in a heap every now and then to take a rest before jumping up and struggling on. It was obvious she wanted to be out walking but it was worrying to see how tired she became after even a small amount of exercise. Some days when we called them for their walk, Leila would jump up from her cushion ready to go while poor Bambi would just lie there, head down, tongue out, looking wistfully after us as we headed off leaving her behind. I don't know if dogs have long-term memory but she seemed to know what she'd be in for if she came along so we didn't want to force her. Other days she'd be totally fine but always, without fail, she'd need to stop and rest every few minutes, puffing and panting her way along the paths and lanes.

Watching Bambi sleep was a pitiful sight with her head hanging down over the cushions and struggling for breath. Our research revealed that breeds such as pugs and French bulldogs that are bred for their flat faces have such small head cavities that the soft palette hangs down, causing all these breathing problems. Bambi's exhaustion after even short walks and her need for frequent breaks then made sense. It wasn't that she didn't want to do all the normal, active things that dogs love but that her poor deformed body wouldn't let her.

She drooled all over her bedding for the same reason so we had to wash it every few days and we assumed the drool would be over the sofas and cushions as well. Perhaps dogs are a bit like children. If they're your own you don't mind their drool and slobber but if not — no way. The same applied to her rear-end issues. For some reason she must have felt a bit of an itch and would swirl around on the living room carpet with her protruding black bottom, something we found particularly unappealing, as did her chronic farting. Again, maybe it would have been fine if she'd been our own pet. Maybe.

She adored Leila and loved jumping on her, draping over her when lying down together, and she followed her everywhere. Poor long-suffering Leila put up with it, only occasionally getting up and moving to higher ground, which is perhaps why she was so keen to jump up on the sofas. But what with the slobbering, bottom swirling, farting and the dog hair covering every sofa and chair, with the exception of one very hard wooden-framed antique, there was simply nowhere comfortable for us humans to sit. They were, however, very well trained when it came to waiting politely for their meals. And because they had a dog flap in the kitchen, we could happily leave them if we wanted to head out for a few hours.

Apart from their health issues, the dogs were lovely. Leila was a dear old thing and poor little Bambi couldn't help the fact that she was a physical wreck. We felt sorry for them both and cared for them as best we could. But between the dogs taking over all the furniture and the floor-to-ceiling books it was starting to feel incredibly claustrophobic. We'd tried spending a couple of sunny afternoons in the back garden but with no outside table and having to resort to balancing our glasses on the edge of the birdbath, as well as keeping a constant eye on Leila's food-nabbing habit, it really wasn't a relaxing experience. So we formed a plan. We'd explore every National Trust site in Oxfordshire and make the best of it, which we did.

As I've said before, if you look hard enough, there's usually a silver lining. Even though we couldn't enjoy the physical space or have any friends to visit, we did discover some unexpectedly good gastro pubs during our walks around the area and enjoyed all that the village had to offer. We made friends at the pubs, chatted with the locals and spent the summer in a part of Oxfordshire where we'd never been and would never have known about if it hadn't been for this dog sit. The village was in a wide valley with a network of streams and ponds to explore. Many of the houses were thatched beauties while others were in the handsome Georgian style. There was a community orchard, playing fields, community huts where cricketers met after their games and musical groups practised, a theatre and an ancient church.

Our weekends away took us to the farthest reaches of Gloucestershire — the area west of Cirencester around Kemble — and into Malmesbury in Wiltshire. These long weekend breaks were even sweeter for being so greatly appreciated and also for taking us off the beaten track. Having to book accommodation at short notice in the height of summer meant we had to look beyond the main towns and thanks to that, we spent the loveliest days of our entire stay at a B&B in Poole Keynes, a tiny village near Cirencester. Our accommodation was in the attic space under the rafters, with our spacious bedroom looking out over the lawns and orchard at the back and a pretty garden on the quiet road in front.

The local walks were very different from the more open spaces in Oxfordshire. This was a green triangle of woods, green fields and tiny villages such as Oaksey, where we met a talkative gentleman visiting his wife's grave at the parish church and who entertained us with a lively history of the graveyard's inhabitants. Then there was a tasty

Sunday lunch at the Wild Duck Inn in Ewen, a half-hour's walk away, where the food was good but outmatched by its gothic, spooky décor. The exterior alone was worth a visit with high yew hedges hiding the pebbly courtyard, a massive clock on the vine-covered wall and a sheltered rear courtyard wedged between the pub back door and wisteria-clad outbuildings.

So with our weekends off duty, day trips to National Trust properties and nearby Oxford, and exploring the village itself, we made the best of what was really just an awkward situation. It was certainly longer than we would have chosen if we'd known earlier about the sleep-depriving bedroom and the space-invading books and dogs, but it wasn't a total disaster. There are just some things you can't anticipate no matter how vigilant you are. And there's always a silver lining, even if it's just the makings of a jolly good story.

18. The Perils of Oz

And so we came full circle. We now had one house swap, multiple house sits and a yearlong rental under our belts. It was time to try out our newly acquired pet-sitting skills and see how Australia shaped up in this low-impact travelling adventure.

It's true: the grass isn't always greener on the other side; though it's hard to get greener grass than that of lush, damp England. But for grass that grows while you watch and for grass that's baked into cookies, NSW's far north coast is the place to be.

We'd arranged our first Australian sit months earlier while in Treignac looking after Scruff and Réglisse. The photos had been heartening but by that time, with lots of hits but also a few misses and close shaves under our belts, we weren't shy about asking all the relevant questions. Were the dogs allowed on the furniture? Did they sleep in the bedroom, or even worse, on the bed? Was there a dog flap? If not, where would they spend their days when we were out? Did they have health issues?

The only question we'd forgotten to ask was if the house was air-conditioned but in the grand scheme of things it seemed fairly unimportant. The house looked crisp, clean and comfortable; its setting in the shadow of the Mount Warning caldera was awesome; the owners, Greg and Carla, were good humoured and down to earth; and anyway, we'd always resisted air conditioning in our efforts to be environmentally responsible so we weren't fussed.

So *of course* the house had no air conditioning, and *of course* we were there at the height of summer during one of the worst heatwaves on record.

All was fine the afternoon we arrived. Greg and Carla gave us a heroic welcome starting with cool drinks and sandwiches on their extensive veranda where we basked in the views of Mount Warning and the creek beyond.

After our long drive we were just starting to relax when suddenly Greg jumped up, dived behind the sofa where we were sitting and starting bashing away with a broom. Grabbing a plastic bag from the side table, he dived back down and after a bit more scrabbling about, finally held the contents aloft — two writhing cane toads.

Being cane toad virgins, it dawned on us that we'd been sitting there for at least a couple of hours, totally oblivious to their existence. We followed Greg into the garage where he kept an old freezer and he instructed us on how to deal with them, which was fairly straightforward. Bag them, stick them in the freezer where they'd painlessly expire and when we had enough to make a decent pile, chuck them into the garbage bin. Trapping cane toads wasn't anything we'd ever considered doing on a pet sit but willing to try anything, within reason, and with this being 'the bush' and us being lowly city slickers, we understood we could increase our bush cred by learning the cane toad ropes.

After that excitement we settled back with our now not-so-cool drinks on the veranda, furtively listening for any rustling behind the sofa, before heading off to enjoy a pint at the historic pub in the nearest village of Tyalgum. We were in luck, it being a busy Friday night, so we met many of the locals, including the butcher, a very plump man who insisted we call him by his cheeky nickname, Tubby. This jolly evening could have gone on and on, with the beer flowing and crispy hot chips magically appearing while we made new friends and heard all the local gossip. Guidebooks pale in comparison to what you can learn by chatting with locals over a glass or two. We were given directions to the best river swimming hole, tips on what to do if stranded in a flash flood, and how to score a free Sunday lunch at the nearby Hare Krishna community. But most intriguing of all, we heard whisperings about — the cult.

It wasn't until we got back home that we were able to probe for a bit more information. We'd finally dragged ourselves away from the camaraderie of the pub and were settled back on the now (we hoped) cane toad-free veranda sofa while Carla and Greg barbequed chicken, poured more wine and gave us the lowdown. The cult, also known as the water people, had been around there for years but they didn't live on a compound like the Hare Krishnas. Instead they were embedded within the community and lived in normal houses so it was often hard to know if someone was a member or not. Their main hangout however, was the trendy teashop in Tyalgum where many of them worked. This teashop would clearly be at the top of our list of places to visit.

The evening wore on very pleasantly as we lingered, surrounded by mosquito coils and candles, watching the cane toads take over the darkening lawn and becoming gently acquainted with our two charges, kelpie Whiskey and shaggy Maggie. By this time we were feeling somewhat guilty as our hosts had an early morning flight and they'd spent hours showing us the ropes, taking us out to meet the locals, cooking and entertaining. So we called it a night and awakened next morning somewhat hungover but at least we didn't have to drag ourselves to the airport. Poor Carla and Greg!

Whiskey and Maggie were well trained, apart from Whiskey's occasional attempts to hop onto the veranda sofa, and they slept in the garage. Greg had told us they'd happily stay there until fetched in the morning but Whiskey didn't take well to thunder so if there was a storm, we might have to bring him in. Greg had also told us that Whiskey was mad about chasing sticks, particularly when thrown into the creek at the bottom of the property, but if we wanted to retain our sanity we should keep to a limit of three, briskly brushing our hands to signal the game was over. The property was so extensive that we needed only to walk them around the perimeter, a bit of a struggle after a couple of days' grass growth, and treat Whiskey to a bit of stick throwing down at the creek.

This was all quite pleasant although we did gradually extend the stick-throwing game since Whiskey adored it so much. It was also becoming uncomfortably hot so the creek's cool water and shady banks were a welcome respite. We'd gather a pile of sticks, as Whiskey would inevitably lose them, and throw a stick from the bank into the creek. Maggie would stand in the water watching with keen interest and excitement, although she'd never join in, while Whiskey took a flying leap into the creek, swim after the stick, climb up the bank and dump it at our feet.

After a few days though we realised we should have kept to Greg's rules. It became harder and harder to persuade Whiskey to leave the creek area and stop searching for sticks. We would collect a pile of nice straight ones and wedge them high in the fork of a tree ready for the next day. But he knew where they were and could barely be prised away from gazing imploringly up at them. Sometimes if he'd lost a stick in the creek and we'd indicated we were ready to go, our stash of sticks cunningly hidden away, he'd run off and find a loose tree root to dig up and dump at our feet ready for more fun. We also noticed him becoming a bit aggressive and possessive of his sticks, so being bitten was becoming a real possibility. It was a great lesson in keeping to the owners' rules and maintaining boundaries.

Our first day was hot and from then on, the heat increased daily until the only way to keep relatively cool was to shut every window and door after the dogs' morning walk and head off before the heat became unbearable. The veranda was baking hot from midday till late afternoon and it was equally hot inside so heading off was our best option and anyway, we wanted to explore this lovely Tweed River Valley. With so many picturesque villages around us with equally picturesque names: Limpinwood, Pumpenbil, Tumbulgum and Uki, and the nearest big town of Murwillumbah, we had no shortage of places to discover. The rich volcanic soil and subtropical rainforest made for lush walks while the historic villages, mainly originating from the cedar-getting days, made for pleasant hours poking about and absorbing the tree-change vibes.

Tiny but trendy Tyalgum though was top of our list after hearing all those tales of cults and water people. We knew this neck of the woods was famous for being the heartland of the counterculture lifestyle, with Nimbin its capital. But the existence of the water people cult was something new so we embarked on our first trip to Tyalgum with a frisson of excitement. Would they be kitted out in bonnets, turbans or flowing white robes? Would we be taken for easy marks and seduced into joining up? Would the Main Street be a scene of grass-infused dancing, chanting and bell ringing?

As it turned out, there wasn't so much a Main Street as *the* street, with a park on one side and on the other, an historic but currently lifeless community hall, a craft shop, a heritage general store and the aforementioned captivating teashop. We browsed in the craft shop where I bought some chalk paint for a little table project I had in mind. The manager was helpful and seemed totally normal in the kind of trendy but slightly alternative garb you'd expect in such a shop: jeans and tie-dyed t-shirt.

Then we braved the searing heat once more to walk the few steps to the general store where we bought some tasty-looking lamb gourmet pies. Anything to save us from cooking in that heat. Tubby the butcher, sadly, didn't get much patronage from us. But apart from the cheerful middle-aged shopkeeper dressed in an unprepossessing apron and denim skirt and a chatty young chap eager to discuss his two dogs tied up at the entrance, the place was empty and with not a single sign of any likely cult suspects. Unless of course, the young man's chatter was his subtle way of engaging us in conversation only to entice us into something more sinister.

At last we were ready to check out the tea shop which, as well as the enticing prospect of finally meeting a water person, had a shady veranda where we could sit under a couple of fans and have a cool drink. The teashop was actually a collection of little cottages — teashop, antique store, gin bar — running the length of a long plot of land and with lots of outside seating in little secret gardens. I was so distracted perusing all the lace doyleys, rugged knitted ponchos, and exotic juice and gin menus, that all thought of the water people completely deserted me. The waitresses were young, pretty and dressed in country-style floaty dresses and pinafores. Hmmm…. But they all looked totally normal, happy and healthy so, slightly disappointed, we consigned the cult tales to the interesting but probably past-their-prime, rural-myth basket.

We went back a few times, including a Friday pizza and jazz night, when we settled into a battered sofa beside the bar with a British group playing, gin flowing and not-such-great pizza on offer. But in that heat, as long as someone else did the cooking, the drinks were cold and the music cool, all was well with the world.

Apart from the heat, we suffered another minor disaster when we had a power outage. The night before there had been a thunderstorm that we'd only noticed because of Whiskey's barking and howling. We brought both dogs in from the garage, settled them in the lounge and finally managed to get back to sleep, completely unaware that the storm had taken out the power. When we discovered this in the morning, our main concern was what we'd do if the fridge and freezer started to thaw out. They were full of human food, dog food and frozen cane toads so we were starting to mildly panic at the thought.

Richard searched high and low for the fuse box but to no avail so I sent an SOS email to Carla and Greg, by then somewhere in Tasmania, while Richard headed off to neighbouring properties in search of help. However, what began as a potential disaster, turned out to be a boon. Greg contacted us from Tasmania and told us where the fuse box was hidden, we made friends with the young couple over the road who shared some useful tips on cow maintenance, and we made friends with our South African expat neighbour who later drove over on his lawnmower to invite us for dinner that night.

These country folk really did live up to their reputation of being friendly, helpful and generous but also with loads of interesting tales to spin. This particular neighbour gave us a fulsome account of the ins and outs of cattle breeding, a subject that had been totally missing from our education thus far, and later gave advice on how to remove the stray cow we found wandering about the bottom paddock and blocking our path to the creek. Whiskey and Maggie weren't at all cow-trained so on our first cow encounter Maggie nearly had her head kicked in. His advice was to wait a day or two and the cow might eventually return to wherever she came from, which was most likely the other side of the creek. And lo and behold, much to our relief, the next day she was gone.

After our slight disappointment at finding no visible sign of water people, we thought it was about time we visited notorious Nimbin, where we felt fairly certain we might at least catch sight of some 'rainbow' people. Attracted by the area's spectacular landscape and its Age of Aquarius lifestyle, we knew that Nimbin was now home to a bunch of ageing hippies and dreadlocked youngsters but we didn't really expect to find anything more than just a normal country town with the occasional tattoo parlour and some shaggy dreads. But this time we were not disappointed. Nimbin exceeded all our expectations. Never had we seen so many psychedelic shop signs, rainbow-decorated gates or racks of cheap flower-power clothing. We drank great coffee, ate healthy homemade cake, were offered hemp cookies and simply luxuriated in the upbeat, laid-back ambiance of the town.

My sister had told me of a friend who'd come back from Nimbin harbouring a tapeworm. While ingesting the tapeworm might well have had nothing at all to do with Nimbin and was just a coincidence coupled with bad luck, Richard also returned with a strange ailment. The morning after our day in Nimbin he awoke to find his ear had turned tomato red and had almost doubled in size. We immediately thought of poisonous spiders or some other such perilous creatures. So off we went to the district hospital in Murwillumbah where the admissions staff seemed to be more interested in his daily alcohol and recreational drug intake than why his ear was the size and colour of a tomato. But then, we *were* in hippy heartland. The doctor gave him a course of antibiotics and we assumed all would calm down.

The next morning though, his ear was even redder and bigger with the swelling covering half his face, which now had erupted in tiny white blisters. So off we went to the hospital once again. Although we were in full panic mode, nobody there seemed particularly fussed. He was taken to the emergency department, where the staff seemed unexpectedly chilled, put on a bed and attached to an antibiotic drip. After testing his renal function, the nurse gave him an even stronger drip, all the while laughing, joking and having a jolly good time. It was the most pleasant hospital visit either of us had ever experienced. To this day we still have no idea as to what caused his ear to swell so badly. However, it brought home how delicate we really are and how easy it is to be brought down by some tiny spider, insect or infection. And it was a great lesson from the hospital staff in how to keep calm and carry on.

So apart from the unrelenting heat, Richard's ear, cane toads, rogue cows, cults, cannabis and then *me* ending up in another hospital's emergency department after being whacked in the leg by the car door on the drive home, we had a wonderful time on the Northern Rivers, and have Richard's scarlet ear photos and my hospital crutches to prove it.

Our second Australian housesitting adventure, again in the hottest month of February, was on a wooded acreage in Kenmore just outside Brisbane in Queensland. We'd met owners Geoff and Marlene while we were all in England a few months earlier so we'd already had a chance to get to know each other over coffee in the historic market town of Cirencester.

Their home sat way back from the road in the middle of bushland and overlooked a man-made pond, or dam as these are called in the bush, in the foothills of Mt Coot-tha. Having already met, we could dispense with the preliminary chat and got straight to a quick run-down on what we needed to do while they were away — mainly plant watering and bird feeding — and then headed down to the shade of the gazebo on the pond for a cool glass of wine. Although only a half-hour's drive from Brisbane, we felt as if we were way out in the wilderness as we sat in perfect silence surrounded by water lilies, ducks and bushland.

Although Geoff and Marlene had a dog, she was so old and infirm that they were taking her on this trip so we had plenty of time, after watering and bird feeding, to explore this area which was totally new to us, even though we'd visited Brisbane many times when visiting our son Andrew. The bird feeding involved doing the rounds of the gardens and bushland around the house dispensing wild birdseed to the local brush turkeys, ducks and sulphur-crested cockatoos and bits of mince steak to the kookaburras and butcherbirds.

Expecting two regular meals a day, these birds began gathering at breakfast time around the back door. The kookaburras would be perched on branches, the cockatoos on the veranda furniture and the cheeky butcherbirds on the kitchen windowsill, while the ducks would be waddling about near the pond and the brush turkeys would be everywhere, digging up the pot plants and rummaging through the garden beds. The moment I opened the back door I'd be attacked by the bolder birds, with butcherbirds being the worst culprits. It was like living through a remake of Hitchcock's *The Birds*, with me as Tippi Hedren, fleeing relentless bird attacks every time I went outside with a lump of mince in my hands.

After a couple of days of this and a bit of research into the pros and cons of feeding native birds, basically all cons from what I could see, we decided to start weaning them off all this seed and mince. Now we knew how unhealthy it was for native birds, especially kookaburras and butcherbirds, to eat pure muscle meat such as mince that discouraged them from finding their own food with all the bones, sinews and other bits they needed to thrive, it became difficult to continue down that path. Some of these birds too could be quite destructive. We knew the cockatoos had been chewing through the outside furniture but we also noticed a few of them on the roof, which gave us a bit of insight as to why Marlene had been complaining about leaks in the attic. All this feeding only encouraged them to hang about waiting for handouts — and to get busy on the roof when they grew a bit bored.

It didn't take long to find a local coffee shop, the historic Brookfield General Store, which also became our regular lunch and dinner spot. We quickly fell into a pleasant routine starting with the early morning bird-feeding frenzy followed by coffee under the General Store's pergola while chatting with local dog walkers. Then we would do a little afternoon sightseeing before returning home for more bird feeding and a leisurely sundowner by the pond. This was our favourite time of the day, that magical hour when the heat died down, the ducks splashed across the water to their roosting beach, the birds settled into the branches — and just before the mosquitoes attacked in full force.

Once that dreaded buzzing started up, it was time to drain the last of our gin and tonics and head back to Brookfield General Store, which by night was transformed into a funky pizza and rib joint. Again sitting outside, we could enjoy excellent food cooked by the American/

Australian couple who owned the place, compare notes about life back in the US and listen to rhythm and blues.

One evening Andrew and our grandsons visited and brought along their rescue dog, Daisy. As usual, we started at the gazebo, which had a floating pontoon attached. Poor Daisy, who'd led a miserable life before her rescue and didn't have a clue about water, gave us a shock when she stepped off the pontoon into the earth-coloured pond and sank like a stone. Luckily she was still on her lead so we managed to haul her out, albeit with much rocking and rolling of the pontoon. Then none the worse from her shock dunking, she gave herself a good shake and ran off after the ducks on their narrow roosting beach — though now keeping well clear of the water. She seemed to have made a full recovery by the time we got to the General Store so while we sat at our rough wooden table eating pizza, she was cheerfully checking out the local canine talent.

About halfway through our languid week in Kenmore, while I was opening the bedroom curtains and Richard was in the bathroom, I heard a very loud crash. Being out in the bush and with all those cockatoos around, my first thought was that either a branch had fallen on the roof or those cockies were up to their tricks. They were very adept at climbing onto tables and throwing things about. One morning I'd found the outside place mats completely chewed through and strewn across the veranda.

Looking out the window I couldn't see any damage and when I checked the veranda all seemed clear there as well. I came back inside just as Richard was leaving the bathroom. He'd heard the noise too so it was clear we needed to investigate further.

Between the bathroom and bedroom was a hall with a door to the garage so Richard unlocked it to check if anything odd had happened in there.

Oh, he said, there's a can on the floor. It must have fallen off the shelf.

Mystery solved and relief all round.

But after a long pause, he said quietly, though with an ominous hint of urgency — Carol, give me your phone. I need to take a photo of this.

He'd lent down to pick up the can and was about to replace it, only to find himself staring straight into the eyes of a whopping great python. It was draped over three shelves, writhing among all the bottles, jars and tools, with its head poking right through a can-sized chink.

That was it for me. I loathe snakes. I can barely even touch a photo of one in a magazine. There I was, standing right at the garage door just a few feet from a creature I'd normally avoid like the plague. I threw my phone at Richard, backing down the hall as far and as quickly as I could.

Richard is fine with snakes. He'd grown up in Florida with his mother occasionally bashing them over the head in their back yard, so he calmly took a photo and then followed me inside, shutting the door firmly behind him. I never did go back into the garage although Richard happily wandered around it a couple of times a day, checking the snake's whereabouts.

It didn't appear again; not that it was any consolation, as we had no idea where it had come from or where it was now lurking. Richard did notice that the hatch to the attic was open so it had either been under the roof all along and had dropped down onto the shelving or it had come in from the bush through the open garage door and was starting to make its way up the shelving into the attic.

Whichever it was, I gave the garage a very wide berth from then on and kept well clear of the hall door.

19. Max of Molly's Farm

A few weeks later in the relatively cooler month of April, we found ourselves once again driving up to the Northern Rivers of NSW and the hamlet of Dorroughby in the subtropical wilderness of the Nightcap Ranges. The name alone was intriguing, with a hint of romance but also danger. 'Nightcap' isn't far removed from 'nightshade' with all its deadly connotations.

This time we'd be caring for an interesting assortment of fins and feathers but for once, no fur. Owners Ray and Colleen had told us we only needed to feed a few goldfish, some chooks, guinea hens and a duck. We would be staying in a cottage they had set up for short-term rentals but we could use their house whenever we wanted.

The area wasn't exactly new to us as we'd already spent those weeks in Tyalgum on the other side of the ranges but this Nightcap spur would be new territory. The beaches around Byron Bay weren't far off and the lush hinterland was full of interesting little villages with all kinds of arts, crafts and local produce. All in all, it sounded like an ideal house sit.

We arrived the afternoon Ray and Colleen were about to set off for Bali. Where else? This area was, after all, the beating heart of the counterculture. And where else would hippies, ageing or otherwise, go on holiday if not to Bali?

As it was school holidays we'd assumed that Ray and Colleen had children that they were taking off for those couple of weeks so it was a surprise when a more mature couple greeted us. And what a fabulous couple they turned out to be. While Colleen served us a very welcome cup of tea, she told us how her mother had moved up here when she was a child, joining the environmental protest movement in the late '70s when rainforest logging was decimating the Nightcap Ranges. As with so many other people we've met, they'd stayed on and created the vibrant hippy, merging into relatively well-heeled artisan, lifestyle we see today. From the dreadlocks and hemp cookies of Nimbin to the crumpled pale linen shirts and kale smoothies of Byron Bay, those first baby-boomer protesters had made their mark.

After tea they took us on a tour of the farm, starting at the newly planted saplings they hoped would replenish a patch of land previously cleared for farming. I was beginning to admire the green credentials of this couple more by the minute.

We then inspected the generously sized chicken coop, tropical fruit orchard and kitchen garden, finishing up at Max the duck's bachelor dwelling: his own cosy hut with water dish, plenty of clean straw and a door he could push open himself when ready to head out at dawn.

Our cottage was beautifully fitted out with all we'd need for cooking, eating and sleeping, and was surrounded by lush gardens planted in tropical reds, pinks and oranges. Colleen had even provided us with steaks and chicken for barbequing, salad and new potatoes, a huge basket of tropical fruit from the orchard and some newly laid eggs. But more on those deceptive little beauties later.

Their own house had been a labour of love. Beginning as a simple cottage, it had evolved over the years into this now sprawling but impeccably organised homestead, named after their granddaughter Molly.

The interior was cool and comfortable with most of its rooms opening onto decks decorated with quirky pottery, incense burners and chairs covered with Indian cotton spreads. During those cooler autumn days we'd spend the late afternoons on the biggest back deck enjoying a pineapple rum toddy, surrounded by a ring of mosquito coils and watching Max the duck rooting around on the lawn below as he waited for his afternoon slice of bread.

Each day of our magical two weeks began and ended with Max. First thing in the morning Richard would head outside to check if Max had emerged from his hut and to feed him his morning bread. This he started to do by hand, morsel by morsel, so that by the time we left, Max wouldn't eat it any other way. Chunks thrown on the grass were ignored as he waddled closer, head bobbing about looking at our hands for his next piece. Ducks' beaks feel a lot like hard plastic as we discovered on the few occasions when Max chomped down on our fingers instead of the bread.

We'd then divide the duties with me feeding the goldfish and then organising breakfast, usually eggs as we had a lot to get through, while Richard and Max made their way through the damp morning grass for the daily chook feeding and egg collecting. This was becoming a first-rate education in fowl husbandry. Apart from the five hens at the stables in England the year before, we'd had little experience with poultry.

We discovered the literal meaning of the term 'pecking order' as we watched how the stronger hens dominated the weaker by hogging the feeder and roosting in the best spots. And as for 'hen pecked', we saw, much to our surprise, how the guinea fowl turned out to be the bosses of the coop, chasing and pecking any hen that was in their way. They ignored the poor old rooster, who was given a certain amount of deference by the hens, but even then a couple of the bossier ones would push him aside if a piece of bread was in the offing.

We had a sad experience with the guinea fowl though. After the morning feeding ritual we'd usually drive to one of the many villages or towns nearby, including that day back in Nimbin where I had my book-writing epiphany. It was on our second morning that we drove off, only to find a dead guinea fowl lying right in the middle of the road.

Richard stopped to check it out but it was clearly dead, so he slung it to the side of the road where we could inspect it at greater length on our return. It had vanished by the time we got back so we weren't able to investigate further, but we also didn't know if it was one of ours. We'd only just arrived and hadn't thought to do a head count.

I emailed Colleen to ask if she had five or six guinea fowl, hoping she'd say five as that was how many we could find. No such luck. Six it was. But not to worry, she assured us. They play chicken on the road all the time. Don't give it a second's thought!

After that we watched the guinea fowl closely and discovered how they would fly in and out of the coop, an ability that set them even further apart from the virtually flightless chickens, and would roam around the garden all day in their little group. Yes, and would sometimes venture to the hole in the hedge that separated this garden sanctuary from the road outside. So at last we found the offending escape — and death — route.

But back to Max. After his morning bread and trip to the chicken coop, he passed his days keeping very close to home and following a very predictable pattern. He'd spend hours at his water bowl, dipping and drinking; then he'd wander over to the chicken coop in search of spare seed and finish back at his hut where he'd quietly return at dusk.

He liked company so when we were home he'd follow us around as we picked fruit from the orchard or tomatoes from the vegetable patch. However, there was a limit to where he'd happily wander. It was as if an invisible fence separated his little circuit from the wider world and beyond that he would not go. He was a true homebody and we became extraordinarily fond of him. As long as he had lots of clean water, a safe bed of straw, food and a bit of human company, he was perfectly happy.

We'd had very little experience with ducks, apart from two ducklings, Daffy and Dinky, that we'd foolishly bought back in the '70s at a permaculture fair when we imagined creating a back-to-the-earth lifestyle baking duck egg cakes, weaving macramé plant hangers and growing bean sprouts on the kitchen windowsill.

The reality was that those cute ducklings quickly metamorphosed into aggressive, very large male ducks so the sprouts I'd grown for our salads to be merely shared with the ducks ended up entirely as duck food. And the larger the ducks grew, the more they consumed so what with being overwhelmed by the increasing number of sprout jars filling my tiny kitchen, running the duck-nipping gauntlet each day on my way across the lawn to the carport and clearing up all the mounds of duck poo now overtaking our small suburban garden, the good life was becoming worse by the day.

We felt sorry for them though, being literally ducks out of water, so Richard built them a little pond made of spare bricks and an old shower curtain at the end of the garden but they soon outgrew that. We even tried getting them into our bathtub once but that created a carpet-soaked mess that took hours to dry out.

Our one attempt at taking them for a swim in the harbour at the bottom of our road was both embarrassing and just too hard to repeat. We'd managed to get them into a box with sides high enough to keep them enclosed but wasn't too awkward to carry.

Off we set and had only just started to cross the road when a car stopped to ask for directions. What the driver made of Richard pointing the way with one hand while clutching a box of nipping, squawking ducks with the other, boggles the mind. However, we finally did make it to the water's edge, let the ducks out and watched them poke about for a while but annoyingly, they were reluctant to get more than a webbed toe wet.

Just then and for the first time ever, we saw a massive white albatross fly by and land just beyond where we were standing. I fervently prayed that the ducks would adopt it and depart, never to be seen again.

No such luck! So with it now becoming abundantly clear that we were stuck with our own double albatrosses hanging round our necks, we did what countless others in our position have done and much to our shame, carried them off under cover of darkness to the duck pond in Sydney's Centennial Park.

We've since been told that ducks disposed of in this manner usually meet a grim fate as they battle with all the other ducks competing for such limited space and food on the pond. But we consoled ourselves knowing that the alternative offered by friends to take them off our hands, or rather from around our necks, while murmuring about the delights of duck à l'orange, might have been far worse. After all, we knew they were pretty aggressive and if they stuck together, who knows what conquests they might have made? Even today their offspring might be roaming free and reigning proudly over Centennial Park's duck pond.

At least Colleen and Ray would never have to worry about whether Max ended up being king of the duck pond or cannibal duck dinner — or flattened on the road beyond their hedge. Max would happily see out his days waddling between his hut, the water dish and the chicken coop, way too old and tough to ever become duck à l'orange.

Only one thing really interfered with our wonderful two weeks on the Northern Rivers, an area that now seemed like our second home, and that was a gastric attack.

Whether it was caused by the overload of free-range eggs that we'd been consuming in an effort to keep the constant supply at bay or the overload of fruit from the orchard — passion fruit, dragon fruit, limes and lemons galore — I came down with such an appalling case of the runs that I was too frightened to eat and couldn't face an egg for weeks afterwards.

We were heading home and staying overnight in the small town of Bellingen but with it being a weekend, there was no pharmacy open so I had to forego what looked like a delicious barramundi dinner at the local pub, judging from Richard's plate, and wait it out until the shops opened the next morning.

Like Max, home seemed to be the safest and healthiest place to be — at least for a while.

20. Final Thoughts

House sitting and swapping have proved to be great ways of trying out different life styles — not quite living in other people's shoes but in their homes and in their communities. Neither is a totally liberating way to travel because there's the burden of caring for homes, gardens and pets; negotiating with strangers and having to manage the occasional trying situation. However, the benefits have certainly outweighed the drawbacks.

There are so many elements that have combined to make our experiment a success that it's hard to know where to start. However, a model that I find useful is based on psychologist Abraham Maslow's hierarchy of needs. This theory has been around for decades and has its critics as well as its flaws but when I look back over all our journeys, it seems to provide a pretty good road map. The main idea is that the lower level needs, those things necessary for our survival, must be satisfied before we're able to fulfil our higher level needs — things like achievement, self-respect and creativity.

The most basic needs are for shelter, order and stability. For house sitters and swappers this is the most important level of all, being about the standard of the accommodation as well as how much work would be required to maintain it.

Here are four tips for maximising your chances of securing a successful sit or swap, for preparing your own home and for helping you cope with whatever the reality turns out to be.

1. Know what you want

When it comes to arranging a house sit or swap, it's vital to be brutally honest with yourself as to both your expectations and also your limits when it comes to these basics. I've said a lot about what we've loved in many of the homes where we've stayed: well-designed renovations, creative décor, comfortable furnishings, beautifully maintained gardens, well-trained pets. But I'm also aware that I've had some criticisms that many people might find nit-picky or just plain mean.

Remember, house swapping and house sitting are transactional arrangements. In a swap, you're hoping for an equal exchange regarding the quality of the accommodation and any extras such as the availability of a car. With house and pet sitting you're doing a job, without payment, that requires you to live in a strange home and perform various duties such as pet feeding, litter box cleaning, dog walking and perhaps gardening or home maintenance so it's important that the home meets (or better still, exceeds) your standards. The owners save a packet in cattery or kennel fees, their homes are protected from thieves and their gardens from desiccation, while you get to try living rent-free in a completely different location, in comfort.

Now it's the 'in comfort' bit you have to work out for yourself and that's why it's important to be clear in your own mind about what you'd be happy living in before taking up an offer. At this stage of our lives, we now only consider homes that are well designed (especially the bathrooms); have orderly, easy-to-manage kitchens; are relatively uncluttered and have at least a queen-sized bed. We prefer no more than a couple of pets — with their own sleeping quarters — and in the case of dogs, trained to keep off (most) of the furniture.

Back in my backpacking, youth hostelling days, I was perfectly happy sleeping in a bunk room, sharing a bathroom with dozens of other girls and putting up with the manager's Alsatian pooping all over the breakfast room floor each morning. That was the scene in Paris where I spent my first few days hostelling but at the time I simply thought it was a bit odd and otherwise couldn't care less. Perhaps if I'd been applying for pet sits then I'd not have turned my nose up at kitchens with magnet-encrusted fridges, sinks full of dirty dishes and floors cluttered with toys, feeding bowls and litter trays. I might not have sniffed at the sight of soggy towels strewn around bathrooms or faded orange and purple duvets crumpled over saggy beds.

But now, it's a different story. I need calm, harmonious and aesthetically pleasing (to me) surroundings. I've tried Hamptons symmetry and pale neutrals in Haslemere; exotic saffron yellows, limes and crimsons in High Hope Barn; simple country-style pine and cane in Dorstone — and have loved them all. But what I now avoid like the plague is any hint of jumble or disorder, out-of-control gardens or animals, and floor-to-ceiling mountains of books. So, how to best ensure you meet those basic needs in any house sit or swap?

2. Do your research

Firstly, ask for photos, as many as possible, especially of the rooms where you'll be spending most of your time. The Goring house exchange photos appealed because the layout and décor of the rooms were very similar to ours, a kind of light Scandinavian simplicity. With enough photos there are no surprises — although there can be exceptions — as happened with our Oxfordshire dog sit. Let's say, the surprise factor is reduced but not totally eliminated.

Secondly, meet your fellow exchangers or pet owners online or in person. That way you'll quickly find out if you're on the same wavelength, if they seem the sort of people who'd look after your home (when swapping) and if their home might be one where you'd be comfortable living for some time.

3. Get organised and become a minimalist

These two really go together if you're contemplating house swapping on a regular basis. The reasons are simple. It's far easier leaving your home if there isn't much work required preparing for new occupants. It's also easier for those new occupants to settle in if cupboards, surfaces and fridges are mostly clear and everything is easy to find. And it's nicer to return to a home that's pretty much as you left it. The naturalist maxim to 'leave nothing but footprints' could apply here, though the odd little gift never goes astray. This all takes some planning but it's well worth the effort.

If I'm going on a particularly long exchange I start running down my food supplies about two months in advance. Then by the time we leave, the freezer is empty of anything but always-useful ice cube trays and the pantry has lots of empty shelves except for a few packets of welcome dry goods such as pasta, rice and sugar. Take this as a great opportunity to clear out your wardrobe, utility room and garage. Cull what you don't need, simplify by buying just a few multi-purpose products and organise them so they're highly visible and stored in places where they'll be used.

As for managing in someone else's home, whether a sit or swap, I usually select a few pieces of crockery and cookware to keep on the kitchen counter and simply reuse those. I often keep my food stash on the counter as well, rather than risk losing track of everything in the pantry, especially on short sits. Becoming an organised minimalist might entail compiling a file of a few easy-to-prepare dishes that don't need lots of different ingredients, especially herbs and spices, or different types of cookware. My own little recipe book includes dishes like spaghetti bolognaise (no surprises there) and chilli con carne, both of which are easily cooked in batches and can be served with pasta, rice or as a baked potato filling. Other suggestions are one-dish fish and chicken bakes that are great with salads, rice and couscous.

Another benefit of a manageable recipe repertoire that requires only a limited number of pots, pans and ingredients is that when it's time to depart, there isn't much to clean up and very little in the way of food to dispose of. I doubt if many people would object to the odd can of tomatoes or packet of pasta being left behind but no one wants to return home to a fridge full of obscure leftovers and half-used sauces.

To summarise: Keep your menus simple, don't buy too many products or ingredients and leave the home in the same state as you found it, if not better.

4. Take a chance on trust
So many friends have asked how we could possibly take the risk of having someone else in our home and driving

our car. Our answer is this — sure, it's risky. We could come back to a ruined wreck or a crime scene with our identities and valuables stolen. These are real possibilities. Or we could do nothing and miss this chance. We could do a Max and stay safely at home, or we could leave our comfort zone and have a Merlin adventure. We could take a chance on human decency and reach out, or fear the worst and withdraw.

So far we haven't been disappointed in our choice, having suffered only one broken wine glass, admittedly one of my best, and a few dead plants. We've noticed on our travels that some people keep a locked filing cabinet or even a room containing their private papers and valuables but this has been the exception rather than the rule. Just take sensible precautions for safeguarding your most treasured things (such as your favourite wine glasses) and don't stress about losing the odd pot plant.

Next in importance are those needs concerning our psychological and emotional well-being: the need for friendship, respect and self-esteem. In my early twenties all these were totally important and I'd have willingly sacrificed a bit of physical discomfort — things from the first level — rather than miss out on being included in the group. As I've said already, Maslow's hierarchy is not perfect. In those days we won respect by sharing tips on how best to travel on the cheap: finding the most comfortable youth hostels; scoring good but cheap meals; knowing the best overnight train trips to save on accommodation costs. Now, decades on from doing

Europe on $5 a day, I've made a couple of useful discoveries about friendships, travel and life in general.

Firstly, no matter what your age, you can always make more friends. If you go through life being open to learning new things and being around different people, you can't help but change — in your thinking, opinions and sometimes even your values — and sometimes that means shedding some friends through their choice or your own. But it also means you can make new ones and that has been one of the greatest and one of the most unexpected benefits we've experienced from house sitting and swapping.

Secondly, life runs more smoothly if, after making these new friends, you make the effort to maintain them. Not only is it pleasant having such warm friendships but it's also easier for organising regular house sits, thus benefitting both sitters and owners. The sitters already know the ropes as far as the house and pets are concerned and the owners are saved the trouble of finding someone new. For example, one couple, Hannah and David, whose home we've now cared for a few times, keep in touch fairly regularly so organising a future sit is quite simple. They live in a comfortable, spacious family home in Berkshire, our old patch. This arrangement has been easy for them and it's been nice for us to slot back into a familiar neighbourhood when our time frames align.

We've been lucky too that in many of our house sits we've been able to have friends or family join us either to stay overnight or just visit for a day, another benefit of building a good relationship with the owners. Our son Andrew stayed with us for a couple of weeks in Berkshire, which worked well for us all. We knew exactly what the accommodation would be like and how it would truly enhance his experience. Coming from a tiny city flat, he embraced the novelty of waking up to birdsong, heading across the lawn and jumping the ditch to pick his breakfast apples from the old apple tree. And of course, being close to our old home, we could visit our friends but also entertain *them* for a change in the sunny conservatory while enjoying views of the gardens and horse paddocks beyond.

Friendships too, like house swaps and house sits, are reciprocal arrangements. Since our friends always entertain us whenever we return to the UK, this way of travelling has made it possible for us to reciprocate. And there is yet another unexpected benefit. The very act of reciprocating while living in someone else's home forces us to develop news skills in food gathering and cooking that go a long way towards meeting our esteem needs! Whenever we prepare a meal for our visitors on a tricky Aga, or suggest a walk across a muddy cow paddock in some place they've never been, or pick a few stalks of rhubarb for them to take home, we earn a little bit of respect and boost our own self-esteem. Certainly unintended but consequential, at least in a small way.

For that reason I was very glad that Hannah and David's garden was so abundant, since our friends, who always come bearing gifts of homemade honey or jam, went home with bags of apples, raspberries, courgettes and hopefully, good memories of a tasty new lunch recipe created from ingredients found in a strange kitchen, and a laughter-filled afternoon engaged in a spot of harvesting.

Then we come to intellectual needs — for learning, exploring and understanding the world — and again, for me this has changed over time. In my twenties I wanted to explore all kinds of new places but I was particularly interested in those places I'd studied at university. This meant that although I was happy to roam, relying on my Eurail map and tips gleaned from chance meetings with fellow travellers, I also had a plan: to visit anything related to the Vikings in Scandinavia and to medieval history in the UK. Since my plan focused on sites of historical importance such monuments, museums and galleries, it was actually similar in many ways to regular tourist itineraries, only more targeted on a couple of specialist areas.

But nowadays, with my formal studies and career far behind me, I'm more like Merlin — still free to roam where I want but without any particular purpose apart from whatever piques my interest at any particular time. House sitting and swapping are now ideal ways to travel because so much depends on serendipity. I might have a general idea about where we both might like to go and then simply see if I can find a match. And from that, anything can happen.

When we decided to rent in England for a year, we wanted to be within a couple of hours' drive from our friends but even that limitation still offered a lot of scope. No longer having to commute to London each day meant we didn't have to live on a train line and so could look for house sits in areas we'd never contemplated before. That freedom led to our pet sits in the semi-rural countryside of Berkshire and windy Brill, and once we'd lined up our rental property for a few weeks down the track, allowed us to head even further afield.

With our house-hunting mission accomplished, we had plenty of time to roam anew, from pet sits in the woods of the Vendée to the dry olive groves of Andalucía, discovering new places and people along the way. I hadn't been particularly interested in learning about these areas until, through this combination of chance and necessity, we simply ended up there. It was sheer chance that these assignments turned up at just the right time when we needed somewhere to stay for a few weeks. But once there, and because of the places we passed through on the way, our journey became a surprise education in ways that we might well have touched on before but had never explored in depth.

We discovered what it was like to live amongst horses and livestock. We learned of the importance of windmills in pre-industrial England, the history of the slave trade on the French Atlantic coast, and the trauma of the Spanish civil war. We tried living as villagers in Oxfordshire, the Cotswolds and the Welsh Borders. We had a go at some DIY in a crumbling French château and became adept at cooking spaghetti and fruit crumble on an Aga.

Our travels forced us to face the worst in human nature, whether spawned in the fertile breeding grounds of intolerance and superstition or spurred by the lust for blood and treasure: war, persecution, slavery, genocide.

But we also saw the best in human nature: Valencia's gleaming City of Arts and Sciences, the vibrant literature and science festivals of the Cotswolds, and the gentler communities that have emerged in every place we stayed. We were constantly inspired by the magnanimity, reasonableness and just sheer decency of the human spirit when given space to flourish.

Next in importance is the need to be with nature, at least occasionally. As a child I loved playing out in the parks and bush. They were places of freedom, excitement and adventure where my friends and I could exercise our imaginations.

But as I've grown older I've developed a love of nature for the peace it brings to both body and mind. Whether relaxing in the afternoon sun in the harmonious riot of a cottage garden or hiking through a field, pungent with the odour of cow manure and freshly cut grass, the sense of peace and well-being reaches its peak at such times. Those are the moments when I feel something close to awe, whether gazing over silvery Spanish olive groves or the darkening hills of High Hope Barn.

There's one more benefit that this kind of travel brings that also relates to an environmental theme: its modesty and gentleness. No matter how hard we try, we can't avoid having a negative impact on the environment but we can do our best to soften it. The more I've grown to appreciate the natural world, the more I've grown aware of the terrible toll mass tourism has taken on both nature and also on major cities like Venice and Amsterdam, places that are increasingly attractive to an ever-increasing number of travellers.

Travelling this way reduces the impact of tourism by reducing the need for hotel rooms or Airbnb-type accommodation that can devour affordable local housing, while also spreading visitors over a much wider area where tourists might not normally travel. Our most treasured memories now are of the natural world in places we'd never have known about if not for such house sitting and swapping serendipity.

The apex of the hierarchy is about 'self-actualisation': the never-ending quest for personal growth and self-discovery that persists throughout our lives. What this quest entails is different for every person and most likely changes along with new experiences. And because the very nature of this kind of travel leads to so many new experiences, change will inevitably happen.

House sitting in particular has a way of increasing the possibility of chance encounters and unforeseen events. Since the locations are often in off-the-tourist-trail locations and because being part of a different community for a fair amount of time is part of the deal, there's much more room for surprise. It's like being offered the opportunity to kick-start the process of renewed self-growth by throwing up situations that you might not otherwise choose or would even take pains to avoid.

Is this form of travel for everyone? Not necessarily. Balancing the risks and rewards might not always be straightforward or easy. It's worked for us because Richard has always been more of a Merlin, eager for the next adventure and willing to put up with a fair bit of uncertainty and risk, while I'm more of a Max, content in my own space and anxious about possible mishaps when venturing too far from my comfort zone. House sitting and swapping have allowed us to be both.

Our next trip for example, will have a bit of Max and a bit of Merlin. We'll be swapping with Elaine, a British lady who splits her time between her large traditional family home in the southeast of France and a genteel flat in England's South Downs.

Among the 'knowns' will be Elaine herself and her flat, which we've already visited a couple of times when on a house sit nearby.

What will the 'unknowns' be? Well, that's the whole point. All I do know is that there'll be plenty.

I've already had a hint. When Elaine called us here one wintery Sydney evening while she was roasting in heatwave conditions in France, she revealed a nasty-looking bright red spider bite that she'd just had treated at the local hospital.

Hmmm…. This situation was starting to seem vaguely familiar but with the added potential challenge of trying to communicate with a French doctor rather than a laid-back nurse in Nimbin.

And so to final thoughts. This way of travelling has taught me many valuable lessons but perhaps the most important of all are these: Never stop learning, be open to change, and aim for a balance between staying put and venturing forth.

Wherever nature is cherished, minds are free and hearts warm, there you will find the good life. It's up to each of us to help create this on our own patch but we can also enjoy it for a while on another's.

Yes, we're all in trouble as Trump rants, the Earth heats up and the seas become clogged with plastic. But there are too many awesome people and still-glorious places out there to just crumple in despair and give up on this quest to discover — and live — the good life.

As to whether ours is an example worth following, judging from the riches we've reaped along the way, I'd suggest it's absolutely a path worth trying.

Life goes on at *www.tryinglives.com.*

21. Acknowledgements

My deep gratitude goes to all the following:

Ann Bullon who first suggested pet sitting and got the ball rolling; Anne Maher, Jenny Caddy and cousin Chris Wakeford for encouraging me to move from blog to book; Lisa Kusel, fellow Green School Bali survivor, whose memoir *Rash* was both inspiration and literary model; my sister Heather whose provision of an extensive potential readership among her friends forced me to get my skates on; son Andy for his invaluable, no-holds-barred editorial advice; Barry Edwards for his proofreading expertise; Amanda Asplund for her perfect illustrations; Richard for his companionship, enviable formatting skills and uncomplainingly getting up in the cold for early morning dog walks; perfect homeowners and fellow exchangers: Pamela of Cheltenham, Elaine of Chichester, Christine and Robin of Bath, now all firm friends; and everyone, both human and animal, mentioned in this book — although not always by their true names.

Notes

I found our house sitting assignments through TrustedHousesitters.

My house exchange company of choice was Home Base Holidays: *www.homebase-hols.com*.